*To my late Brother
Robert Elwyn Turner
Solicitor, of Ludlow
who died in 1940 while serving
with the King's Shropshire Light Infantry*

Acknowledgements

Many people have helped me over the years that I have researched the life and work of Joseph Murray Ince but I would particularly like to thank Col. Gerry Blyth (for lifts to the National Museum and Gallery of Wales at Cardiff), Dr. H. Connor of Hereford, Revd. Richard Hart of Beguildy, Mr. Bob Jenkins of Kington, the late Mr. R.C.B. Oliver, M.J. Petty M.B.E., M.A. (Cantab), Frank Rose and Dr. D.M. Rose, and Dr. Schofield, together with the staff of many libraries, museums and galleries including those at The National Gallery, The British Museum, The Fitzwilliam Museum, The National Museum and Gallery of Wales, the National Library of Wales, The Victoria and Albert Museum, Eton College, Leominster Museum, Hereford Museum and Library, The Ashmolean Museum, Presteigne Library (particularly Margaret and Coral), staff at the Archives in both Hereford and Powys, and the Association d'Entrade de la Noblesse Française in Paris. Sincere thanks go also to all my friends and neighbours who have given me much encouragement (and endless cups of coffee) over the years, to those private collectors who have let me look at their paintings by Ince and who have allowed some to be reproduced in this book but who wish to remain anonymous, and to Andy Johnson of Logaston Press who helped bring the book to fruition. However, my greatest thanks go to Nicholas John Benbow M.A. (Oxon), F.C.A., C.I.O.T., a descendant of Joseph Murray Ince's half-brother, Edward Ince Young, who produced the family tree and provided chapter 5 and the Appendix, along with pieces of information used elsewhere in the text.

Joseph Murray Ince
1806–1859

The Painter of Presteigne

by
Margaret Newman Turner

Logaston Press

LOGASTON PRESS
Little Logaston Woonton Almeley
Herefordshire HR3 6QH
logastonpress.co.uk

First published by Logaston Press 2006
Copyright © Margaret Newman Turner 2006

ISBN 1 904396 54 2

Typeset by Logaston Press
and printed in Great Britain by
The Cromwell Press, Trowbridge

Front cover illustration:
Joseph Murray Ince, attributed to David Cox
Rear cover illustration:
Hay-on-Wye and the Brecon Beacons

Contents

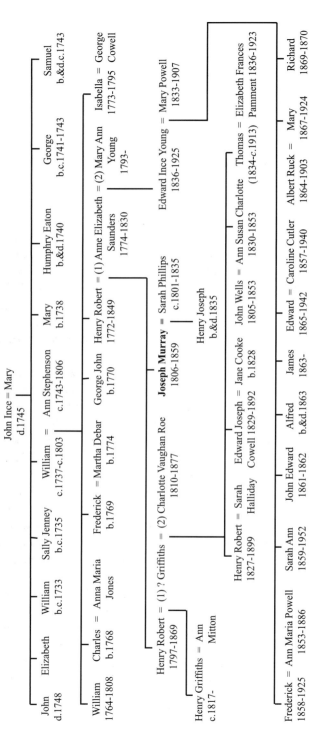

John Ince = Mary
d.1745

John
d.1748

Elizabeth

William
b.c.1733

Sally Jenney
b.c.1735

William = Ann Stephenson
c.1737-c.1803   c.1743-1806

Mary
b.1738

Humphry Eaton
b.&d.1740

George
b.c.1741-1743

Samuel
b.&d.c.1743

Charles = Anna Maria
b.1768   Jones

Frederick = Martha Debar
b.1769   b.1774

George John
b.1770

Henry Robert = (1) Anne Elizabeth = (2) Mary Ann
1772-1849   Saunders   Young
                  1774-1830   1793-

Isabella = George
1773-1795   Cowell

William
1764-1808

Henry Robert = (1) ? Griffiths = (2) Charlotte Vaughan Roe
1797-1869   1810-1877

Joseph Murray = Sarah Phillips
1806-1859   c.1801-1835

Edward Ince Young = Mary Powell
1836-1925   1833-1907

Henry Griffiths = Ann
c.1817-   Mitton

Henry Joseph
b.&d.1835

Henry Robert = Sarah
1827-1899   Halliday

Edward Joseph = Jane Cooke
Cowell 1829-1892   b.1828

John Wells = Ann Susan Charlotte
1805-1853   1830-1853

Thomas = Elizabeth Frances
(1834-c.1913)   Pamment 1836-1923

Frederick = Ann Maria Powell
1858-1925   1853-1886

Sarah Ann
1859-1952

John Edward
1861-1862

Alfred
b.&d.1863

James
1863-

Edward = Caroline Cutler
1865-1942   1857-1940

Albert Ruck = Mary
1864-1903   1867-1924

Richard
1869-1870

Ince Family Tree.

Space does not allow for inclusion of all the offspring in each generation

viii

Introduction

It was the plaque under the north wall of St. Andrew's Church, Presteigne, that became the focus for this book. Written in the flowery English of the time — some of it inaccurate, it still had an ability to rouse the senses — and to question further. Who was this artist? There seemed to be very little known about him, even locally. Nothing in the guide book; and the blue plaque on Roseland, the house where he had lived, had his name mis-spelt! Neither in the *Oxford Dictionary of National Biography*, nor in those by Cust or Redgrave do the details appear correct. Mr. R.C.B. Oliver, the historian from Llandrindod Wells, did some valuable research — but it certainly only contributed partly to an understanding of the artist's career.

The church plaque is right when it refers to the deep feeling and love Ince had for landscape — but when we come to the part 'content to abandon the exciting and hazardous struggle' — it veers from the truth, for an artist who exhibited prolifically for two decades or more — 197 paintings in all, and 16 hung in the Royal Academy — he was selling so well, and on commission, he would not have needed to exhibit in his later years. It is only after his death we see his works submerged by the great tide of Victorian paintings, and the Impressionists.

My trail started with the big museums. One soon learnt that having a transparency made from a painting was costly business! At the same time as researching Ince it made sense to follow up with John Scarlett Davis (1804–45) as well, after all they had been lifelong friends. There could not have been more of a contrast. With Ince there was so little to go on, whereas with John Scarlett Davis there were not only 92 letters written by him, but numerous family papers. It was because of this abundance hat, after lecturing on him several times, I decided not to write the biography, but passed it on to the able pen of Tony Hobbs.

However, tenacity was rewarded by several totally unexpected finds. I received a telephone call from Nicholas Benbow, who had been given my number by Hereford Museum. He was a descendant of Dr. Robert Henry Ince. It was known already that Ince had a 'half-brother' — a natural son of the Doctor. Nicholas had never been to Presteigne, but full of enthusiasm to find the family tree — which research gave backbone to the book, and would, to me, have been a necessary duty — he made the visit.

Next, head down in a pile of papers at Powys Archives, I found letters between R.C.B. Oliver and the then keeper of Pictures and Maps at the National Library of Wales, D. Huw Owens, and a copy of a portrait, small, in watercolour backed by a letter of provenance from a great-great-niece of Ince. This was a bequest to Hereford Museum, and they, indeed, did have the original, believed to be by David Cox. The letter made clear that Ince's mother, Anne-Elisabeth, was a daughter of a Comte le Jeune, who was a victim of the French Revolution. She called her son 'Jean-Marie' — but he became 'Joseph Murray as befitting his English father.

The information about the neighbours around Presteigne at the time contributes to the social history of the town at the very end of the Georgian era. It was interesting, too, that, in Wales, parish records are held by each vicar — in England they are at the Archives of the County, far more distant and difficult to access.

Finally, a big breakthrough came with the chance word of a neighbour, that there was a good painting by Ince at Eton College. This was a research in comfort, as a family friend has been Director and Precentor of Music there for over 20 years. The painting was indeed of interest — but a fragment held at the College of a letter written by Queen Victoria to the King of the Belgians led to further research at Cambridge. When I first spoke to an eminent archivist at Cambridge and told him, diffidently, that I was writing the biography of Joseph Murray Ince, his reaction made all the hard work worthwhile. 'Joseph Murray Ince!' he said, 'Writing his biography?' About time too! — he was absolutely brilliant!'

Margaret Newman Turner
2006

1   Early Life in Presteigne

Sir Lionel Henry Cust was, from 1895 to 1909, the Director of the National Portrait Gallery and from 1901 to 1907 Surveyor of the Kings Pictures and Works of Art. His biographies of several artists in the *Dictionary of National Biography* were praised for their accuracy and painstaking research — and '... made a fresh beginning in the study of English Art.' It can hardly be said, however, that he 'maintained the level of information at the highest practicable standard of fullness and accuracy' in the case of Joseph Murray Ince, who had an account that was rather cursory and, in some respects, inaccurate. We do know he had obtained some information from the Rev. Augustus William West, Rector of Presteigne from 1880 to 1893, but this was long after Joseph Murray Ince had died, may only have been of a private nature and to do with the 'Young' branch of the Ince family who were still living in Presteigne at the time. It may be that Sir Lionel was depending too much on Redgrave's *Dictionary of Artists of the English School.*

Cust maintained that Joseph Murray Ince was born in Presteigne. In fact he was born in London and came down to Radnorshire as a baby.

The War Office lists in the National Archives include, in the Records of the Royal College of Surgeons, Sir Robert Drew's *Commissioned Officers of the Medical Services of the British Army* which was published in 1968 by the Wellcome Historical Medical Library. This records that Dr. Henry Robert Ince, father of Joseph Murray Ince, was born on 12 January 1772. On 17 December 1792 he was examined to be a surgeon in the Militia, but did not pass; he sat the examinations again in February 1793 when he obtained the Diploma of Membership of the Surgeon's Company. This does not point to any degree of incompetence, indeed he was still only 21, and on 15 March of the same year he was appointed Assistant Surgeon to the Royal Berkshire Regiment of Militia,[1] the year that France declared war on Britain. The Berkshire Militia had assembled at Reading in December

1792,[2] at a time of growing tension with revolutionary France. The militia's role was to take responsibility for defence of the realm, specifically to defend the shore against the risk of foreign invasion and to release trained troops from the regular army for service overseas.

The Berkshire Regiment was ordered to the coast of Kent and Sussex in February 1793, remaining in that area for three years. The Colonel of the regiment, ironically in view of the Ince family's later connection with Presteigne, was Lord Radnor, whose seat was in Berkshire. The regiment was posted to Totnes in Devon in the summer of 1796 and remained in the West Country during 1797. Its winter quarters for 1797–1798 were in Bristol and the regiment remained there for much of 1798.

The marriage register of St. James' Church, Sussex Gardens, Paddington, shows that on 30 July 1796, presumably before the regiment's posting to Totnes, Henry Robert Ince Esq. of the Parish of St. James' Westminster, Bachelor, was married to Anne Saunders of the Parish of Paddington by licence, in the presence of Dinah Shiels and Joseph Wotton. The latter was the Verger, and both appear to have often acted as witnesses. It would seem that Dr Ince was of some social standing, an officer and a gentleman, and according to Mr. R.C.B. Oliver, 'it may or may not be significant that no friend or relative of his was present as a signing witness. Ann signed her name in a clear, good hand.' Mr. Oliver seems to suggest that Dr. Ince was marrying 'beneath him'.[3]

However, the discovery of a copy of a letter in the Powys archives throws an entirely new light on the matter. The original of this letter had been 'buried' in the files at Hereford Museum, but has now been found and shows that Dr. Ince had, in fact, married into the French aristocracy. The letter, signed by a Mrs. Dorothy M. Hextall, and dated 7 November 1977, states 'My great-great uncle was Josef-Marie Ince (generally known as Joseph Murray Ince) by which name he signed his pictures, he was a grandson of Comte le Jeune, de Paris, an émigré in the French Revolution'.[4] Mrs. Hextall goes on, 'The Comte's daughter, Anne-Elisabeth married Dr Henry Robert Ince, physician and surgeon (later) of Presteigne'. She writes of David Cox teaching in Hereford and that Joseph Murray had been his favourite pupil. She subsequently bequeathed a watercolour portrait to Hereford Museum, which she stated was of Joseph Murray Ince painted by David Cox, indeed she says that 'Cox D' can be seen 'playfully' signed in the folds of the coat. After examination Hereford Museum have designated it 'attributed to David Cox'.

Mr. R.C.B. Oliver heard about this bequest from the then Curator of Hereford Museum when it was sent there in 1990 and managed to get a copy made, which he sent to Mr. Huw Owen, keeper of pictures and maps at the National Library of Wales, Aberystwyth on 8 June, 1990. It would appear that the original picture was re-framed in order to have it copied, so that any further information on the backing was lost. (Hereford Museum originally assumed that the portrait was actually of David Cox. However the character in the painting had obviously gone bald fairly early — say in his 30s — and examination of another portrait of David Cox shows that he had a good head of hair when in his 60s! The latter's bone structure is also very different, Cox having a long face and strong features.)

It is hardly surprising that Anne-Elizabeth signed her name Anne Saunders at her marriage to Dr. Ince. She could have taken a name which had some connection with her own family, such as Sands or Sainte, but Saunders was more English and a common enough name. The fear of the efficiency of French intelligence and possible reprisals was not simply fictitious as shown so well by Baroness Orczy and her characterization of the sinister Monsieur Chauvelin in her book, *The Scarlet Pimpernel*. As an émigré Anne-Elizabeth was lucky, she had met and fallen in love with her English Army surgeon and married him in 1796. This was, however, three years after war had been declared on Britain by France in 1793, and patriotic feelings were running high. It is quite possible that she could have met with some slights

Part of the letter written by Mrs. Hextall setting out Ince's French pedigree in society as the initially generous feelings towards the French were beginning to dissipate.

It was during the period that the Berkshire Regiment were based in the West Country that Ince's elder brother, Henry Robert, was born in Wendover, Buckinghamshire, on 3 October 1797 where he was christened exactly a month later.[5] We know from the Will of William Ince, his grandfather, that he had furnished a house in Wendover for the baby's father, after whom the boy was named. It is unlikely that Dr. Henry Ince was able to spend much time with his wife, Ann, during her pregnancy or when his son Henry was a baby.

Army Lists show that Dr. Henry Ince joined the 2nd Battalion of the Coldstream Guards, then stationed in London, as Assistant Surgeon on 16 June 1800. It may have been an attractive proposition for Henry Ince to move his family back to London from Wendover and to carry out his military duties only a short distance from the family home. Whatever the reason for his transfer from the militia to the regular army, (and we cannot rule out simple financial advantage), we do know that Henry Ince retired on half pay from the Coldstream Guards on 29 October 1802, by exchange with a Dr. John Crake. Such a practice was quite normal at the time, providing a way for an officer who had originally purchased his commission to leave the Army. When he made this transaction, Henry Robert Ince would have sacrificed half his pay and the right to sell his commission, in return for the right to give up his military duties and to receive his half pay as a form of pension. In essence, it was a method of getting a pension after ten years of active service. Dr. Ince was lucky — he continued to draw his half pay for the next 47 years! However, prevailing circumstances may have also influenced his decision. The Peace of Amiens had been signed with Napoleonic France in March 1802 and Addington (who had replaced Pitt in February 1801) had embarked on a programme of troop reduction which was intended to reduce significantly the size of the regular army.

The family moved back to London at some time before the birth of Joseph Murray Ince in 1806. William Ince's Will made in 1800 mentions that Henry Ince had already had furniture for houses in Goodge Street and Grafton Street. R.C.B. Oliver noted in his article[6] that in 1805 Henry Ince's address in a list of members of the Royal College of Surgeons was in Upper Grafton Street. Dr. Ince was certainly in London in 1802 as Assistant Surgeon to Invalids at the Tower of London and continued with these duties until 1805. (This was the Hospital for War Wounded Soldiers, similar to Les Invalides in Paris.) It was more than possible that Dr. Ince also had a private practice.

After the birth of their first child, Henry, there appear to have been no more children until Joseph Murray was born in 1806, when the family were living in Upper Grafton Street, but they were clearly thinking of where and how they would like to bring up their family.

It had been a very strange last quarter of a century in England. In 1780 Newgate prison had been burnt down when the felons had been released by the mob. War with France had begun in 1793 and continued since then with the exception of a small break of two years heralded by the Peace of Amiens. In 1798 France had attempted to invade Ireland which caused alarm. Income Tax had been introduced to pay for the war, which was very unpopular. There had been an assassination attempt on George III in 1795, and again in 1800 during a performance of *Figaro* ('his Majesty remained very calm'). The United States of America had proclaimed and won her independence. With the price of bread rising, food riots were frequent. In 1797 there was a serious mutiny in the North Sea fleet. There were frequent cholera outbreaks. On a possible family note, the Spanish and French laid siege to Gibraltar and all would have been lost save for a certain Sergeant Major Henry Ince.[7]

Yet concurrent with all this strife, there was wonderful creative activity and new inventions. The Ironbridge was completed in 1779, the Marylebone Cricket Club was founded in 1787 — 'White top hats with black bands will be worn'! The Royal Institute was formed, canal mania took hold, lighthouses were built, and architects such as Adam and Sir John Soane were busy at work. The steam engine was invented, medicine was advancing, small-pox vaccination was discovered, the slave trade was soon to be abolished and J.M.W. Turner had been elected to the R.A. at the age of only 28. Even so, the war with France was always on the mind. In spite of the naval victories off Ushant, Cape St. Vincent and at the Battle of the Nile, there was always the fear that Napoleon would one day attack England. Martello Towers were built all around the coast and 30,000 volunteers were needed for the army. Rumours were rife, Napoleon was even supposed to be tunnelling under the Channel! The Battle of Trafalgar saved the day at sea, but Napoleon would still have to be defeated on land. It was quite possible that the fear of Napoleon, the start of the Industrial Revolution and all these disparate pressures and problems saved Britain from a more bloody revolution as had occurred in France.

The timing then was just right when Dr. Ince received a letter from his friend from medical school days, Dr. Edward Jenkins, M.D., J.P., D.L, suggesting that he should come to Presteigne as a country practitioner. The two men had known each other at medical school in London and although Dr. Jenkins was eight years older, the friendship had lasted.

Presteigne? — Where was Presteigne? It must have seemed a different world. The very fact that it was in Wales was strange, another country indeed, even if in the diocese of Hereford. Yet here was a part of Britain where farming had been carrying on in the same way for hundreds of years. Where hills were wild and sparsely populated, where there was still a Georgian way of life and the fires and squalor of industrial revolution had not yet reached. It had the dignity of being the county town of Radnorshire where the Crown Court and Assizes had been held for 400 years.

The Jenkinses had deep roots in Radnorshire. We meet them first in the Bleddfa Parish records of 1702 when Griffiths Jenkins, son of Walter Jenkins born in 1677, a yeoman farmer who lived at Ty-Mawr-Yn-Y-Storlin, married Alice, daughter of David Ap Roberts of Glan Llugwy. Their son, David Jenkins, married Elizabeth Duggan of Presteigne and their son, also David, married the widow of Hugh Piefinch of Presteigne. It was their son Edward (who married his step-sister Mary) who had become a doctor. Through the series of marriages the family inherited several farms along the Lugg as well as valuable properties in Presteigne. The original Ty-Mawr, by hearsay a most beautiful Elizabethan house, lasted many years before it was pulled down. Dr. Edwards was the squire of Nant-y-Groes which was the original home of John Dee, that most famous astronomer, mathematician and inventor to Queen Elizabeth I. In 1841 the first census of the nation was taken and the Edwards family, then living in Nant-y-Groes, reads like a Jane Austen novel: there was Mary (Dr. Edward's wife 51, 26 years younger than her husband), daughter Mary 24, Harriet 21, Edward junior aged 17 and Helen 16. Nant-y-Groes was conveniently situated for Presteigne by carriage or by hacking.

By 1841 Dr. Jenkins owned all the land from Bleddfa along the Lugg as far as Nant-y-Groes. The parish register in Bleddfa shows the pews Dr Jenkins had bought for his farms; 'to what place the new pews allotted in the parish church of Bleddfa, no 3 & 4 Edward Jenkins of Cwmgerwin and Llataugue, no 9 Dorluggan and no 18 Llanligo'.[8]

The Jenkinses were indeed an old and respected family and Dr. Ince felt it was the right moment to move.

2   Childhood

It is surprising to learn that the Royal Mail dates back to the reign of Henry III (1216–1272) if only to a messenger of the Court. By the time of Edward I there were stations set up at which horses were kept for those 'riding Post'. By 1482 there was a relay of horsemen established every 20 miles on major routes, payment made by the Treasury. In Henry VIII's reign, there was a Post Centre at the Windmill in Old Jewry in the City of London, which maintained a number of horses, and private letters were beginning to be carried.

It was Charles I who produced a plan to charge for delivery and distance on private mail. This system lasted for 150 years, but the Post boys (and there was actually a girl at Corwen in North Wales in 1792) were often ill mounted, whilst the frequency of robberies and even murder became so bad, that change was needed.

It was a plan by John Palmer, strangely a theatre entrepreneur from Bath, who put forward the idea of special Mail Coaches, each one carrying a Post Office guard, armed with a cutlass, a brace of pistols and a blunderbuss, (who was prepared to guard the Royal Mail with his life). He wore a scarlet coat with blue lapels, gold braided, and a black hat with a gold band.

At this time the major roads were being improved due to the system of turnpike trusts. On 2 August 1784 a mail coach carrying mail and four passengers departed from the Swan Tavern in Bristol, called at the Three Tuns in Bath and arrived at the Swan with Two Necks in London 16 hours later, exactly on schedule. Only once, in 1786, was a mail coach held up by a highwayman, as it entered London, and he was shot dead by the guard! Mail coaches ran strictly to time, were free of tolls, and had right of way over other traffic on the road, the guard carrying a post horn to alert the turnpikes and inns of their arrival. For the privileges of security and speed, passengers were charged more and places were limited to four.

A stagecoach of the type possibly used by the family for the journey to Presteigne, here shown in a flooded landscape

However, the privately run stage coaches were able to carry more passengers and many companies sprang up as vehicles and roads improved. Dr. Ince with his young family to move would have had to choose between the expensive, but fast and secure, Royal Mail; a stage coach; a private carriage, or a post chaise (very vulnerable). One guesses he probably chose a stage coach; whilst roads had indeed improved, they were still often quagmires in wet weather; deep wheel ruts could overturn a vehicle, horses could be injured or go lame, so there was safety in numbers!

The stage coach to Presteigne left Hyde Park Corner at six in the morning, onlookers would gather alongside those (some tearful) saying farewell. It travelled via Hounslow, Henley, Oxford, Chipping Norton, Broadway, Pershore and Worcester. The journey would have taken at least 24 hours, with a change of horses every 20 miles. Maybe the family would have stayed overnight at the Crown or some other inn in Worcester and picked up a later coach the next day, and then, by way of Leominster and a further two or three tolls and turnpikes, at last arrived in Presteigne.

They may have had some heavy items such as family furniture, in which case this would have gone by the old baggage wagon, drawn sometimes by oxen, or by six heavy horses and making a speed of about two miles an hour! (Such a waggon was to become a favourite theme in Ince's paintings.) Lighter baggage was carried by pack horse, as it had been for centuries.

The house which Dr. Edward Jenkins had placed at the disposal of Dr. Ince and his family is at the lower end of Broad Street and now marked with a blue plaque. A well proportioned Georgian building, it had four bedrooms and a further attic room for a servant. There was a garden, with stabling and a coach house at the back. Next to the house on the lower side was a paddock which belonged to Fold Farm and would have been used by Dr. Ince as grazing for his horses and to keep a pony for his sons.

While Joseph Murray was still a baby, his father was having to adapt to a very different kind of medical practice to the one he had had in London. He must have purchased a good horse, preferably a strong sure-footed cob, for many of his visits would be made over rough and rocky ground. The cultivated land would not have stretched as far up the hillsides then as it does now, only the valleys were cultivated, just as high up the slopes as a pair of horses or oxen could pull a plough. Beyond, on the upper slopes, were thick deciduous woodlands, mainly oaks, and higher still, open moorland, hills covered with heather and wimberries, in several places peat bog, this only visible in summer by the white bols of cotton grass and the distinctive bright green of the myrtles growing on top. Yet even on these isolated slopes there were tiny ancient farmsteads and shepherd's dwellings. An urgent summons for the doctor meant a gruelling ride, sometimes at night.

In spite of the wonderful air and environment, scarlet fever, diphtheria, influenza, pneumonia and tuberculosis all took their toll. Childbirth and subsequent complications caused many deaths, or sometimes made the mother an invalid for life. Accidents on farms were usually caused by stock; a bull attacking, a horse kicking out, a boar's tusk ripping open a leg. The good doctor's 'black bag' would have had in it his surgical instruments for amputation, (pain relief in these cases would probably have been brandy!). He would have had Prussic Acid drops for complications in breathing such as asthma and whooping cough; strychnine for paralytic diseases, ipecuana for coughs and croup and as an emetic; extract of gentian for flatulence and indigestion and as a tonic; colchicine for gout; jalop and rhubarb extract for constipation; quinine for fever and aloes as a laxative. Other treatment included blood letting, sometimes with leeches, or blistering with mustard oil to the side of the head, for strokes.

This part of the country was well known for the families of bone setters, a gift handed down through the generations, and still here now.

The doctor would certainly have turned to them. The old beliefs, usually discredited as myth and folklore, are sometimes based on scientific fact (as is now being proved), and there were many wise old people who were well versed in herbalism. They would drink teas and wines of cowslip, dandelion, elderflower, blackberries, camomile, and beech bark for rheumatism, make jelly from mountain ash and crab apples, keep bees for honey, knew that meadow sweet, water mint, and vervain were the herbs most sacred to the Druids.

Even as far back as 1657 William Coles wrote that hedge garlic 'was eaten by many country people as a sauce with their salt fish', in Wales it was fried with bacon. 'Lamb's lettuce' was eaten, as was young ground elder, as a salad, and also cooked; elderberry syrup with honey was a cough mixture, tansy 'cakes' were cooked in Lent. There was also other local produce including a variety of mushrooms and funghi, whilst cider was made on every farm and at harvest time each man's ration was a gallon a day!

There was some lunacy, and more usually than not it was through inbreeding of families in the same valley; people who only travel by walking do not go far to find a mate! But most children who were born with a disability or crippled, tended not to live very long. Life was hard.

In the town the doctor would have visited on foot and would also have owned a gig, possibly a 'Stanhope' or Dog-cart which were becoming popular as they were well sprung for rough roads. Presteigne was conscious of its status and dignity, with its Assizes and Great Sessions and its regular Manorial courts. Nevertheless it always reflected and was influenced by the farming of the surrounding district and supplied those farmers coming in on Market days with nearly all their wants. Added to this the Militia (members of which could now volunteer for the Regular Army) mustered twice a year, thus temporarily increasing the population.

The High Street was a busy thriving work place with bakers, butchers, saddlers, corn dealers, coopers and grocers to name but a few, all with apprentices who could work for the day when they too became owners. There were over 30 inns,[1] albeit that some were simply front room ale houses. Hirelings and post chaises could be obtained from the White Hart on Hereford Street and at the Rose and Crown, and also the New Inn on the High Street. In spite of the fact that the turnpike system had helped raise the quality of roads, only about one tenth of Radnorshire's highways had been improved. There was resentment and violent opposition to paying the tax, particularly as Presteigne was unlucky in that a journey

The tanyard on the Lugg at Presteigne. This c.1920s photograph shows the yard
which was owned by John and Robert Lewis when Ince was a child.
The house of the solicitor, Cecil Parsons, is on the right

to Kington involved paying three tolls: at Corton gate to the Radnorshire
Trust, at Roddhurst gate to the Mortimer's Cross Trust, and at Titley Gate
to the Kington Trust.

Market day was a turmoil of horse drawn vehicles, flocks of sheep and
herds of cattle with the occasional escaping piglet to add to the excitement! Many's the farmer who was 'market-piert' after visiting the inns to
complete a deal, and the best he could hope for was that his horse knew
the way home, and, if in a cart, it did not 'cut the corners' and overturn
him by hitting a gate post! Many of Dr. Ince's accident patients would have
been so caused. Heavy corn and timber wagons were supposed to carry
two drivers, so the one could see if the other went to sleep and fell off,
sustaining a crushed leg from the rear wheel. In the Bleddfa records is a sad
account, but very typical: 'Lewis Edwards, killed near the Stone Bridge on
the Turnpike Road, below the mill on the Saturday night, the 3rd October
between seven and eight, being very dark … it is supposed he fell under the
wagon. The wheel passed over him and he was killed on the spot'.

It was probably in Broad Street that the baby Ince (we shall now call
him 'Ince' as opposed to his father, Dr. Ince, and brother Henry) took his
first toddling steps, and, with his early awareness of colour, shapes, and
movement learn to register in his mind the beauty and the drama of this
unique background of his life. With two intelligent and loving parents and
an older brother to see he was not spoilt, his young life must have been
nearly ideal.

He would soon have realised that one of the most important inhabitants of the town was the blacksmith, and it was here that he must have spent hours; his depiction of horses in his paintings is very accurate, and far better than many of the later Victorian horse painters. That exciting drift of the 'burnt hoof' smell would forever conjure up the scene and the rhythmic 'chink, chink' of the blacksmith's hammer shaping a shoe. 'No foot, no 'oss' as Surtees, through Mr. Jorrocks observed in the book *Handley Cross*. The blacksmith's skill was not only the practical side of taking pressure off a 'sole', or making a shoe lighter or heavier it also included good veterinary knowledge of the diseases of the foot, fetlock joints and leg. On the wall of his parlour would probably have hung the following 'Duties you owe to the Horse' in perfect script, albeit somewhat smoke-stained:

> Up the hill – whip me not,
> Down the hill – hurry me not,
> On the level road – spare me not,
> Loose in stable – forget me not,
> Of Hay and Corn – rob me not,
> Of Clean water – stint me not,
> Sponge and brush – neglect me not,
> Of soft dry bed – deprive me not,
> When tired or hot – leave me not,
> With bit and reins – oh jerk me not,
> When you are angry – strike me not.

The arrival of the stage coach and the sound of the post horn echoing across from the Broad Heath would have set not only the ostlers running but the small boys too, to watch the unloading at the Duke's Arms or the Posting House; stare at passengers, and overhear their hair raising stories! The wild hills between Presteigne and Aberystwyth were the most feared part of the journey, not only from robbers but the weather. A coach had once gone over the steep dingle and hairpin bend just west of the Forest Inn — stories like this were never forgotton.

Occasionally Dr Ince would take his son with him on his visits to local farms. He would also have been free to play with the other boys in the town, and as we shall see there were plenty of large families in Presteigne at the time.

His favourite pastime was fishing, judging from those first wonderful paintings of fishing creels, completed at such a young age (12 or 13) (plates

1-11).[2] It was an interest he retained throughout his life. He would have become absorbed in the peace and quiet of the river bank which meant the start of an acute observation of nature; this was his grounding, this is what draws us to his landscapes, we feel the knowledge, and indeed the love that is there. The Lugg was a larger river than it is now, and full of fish. As a little boy, Ince would have stood in the shallows turning over flat stones to find bully heads and fill his jar with minnows, or caddis larvae, or felt under the banks and had his fingers nipped by crayfish! Besides the prolific brown trout, there were grayling, chub, gudgeon, tench and, lower down, eels to smoke or 'jelly'. He might even have ridden across to the Wye with his father and attempted to go after a salmon. Even if he had no luck, the sight of 'a leap' would have thrilled him for life.

It is more than possible that by this time Dr. Ince would have known about the young artist prodigy in Leominster, John Scarlett Davis, just two years older than Ince; the distance in a pony trap is perfectly feasible, 12 miles, and one does feel that it is during this time that the two boys became friends for life, rather than later on in London. With their shared passion for fishing and painting it would not be surprising. When Ince was only 12, John Scarlett Davis had already obtained his entry to de la Pierre's Art School and gone to London. David Cox, teaching in Hereford, must have heard about this, but it is most unlikely that the Leominster silversmith's son ever went to David Cox for lessons. It would be too far to go daily, and there is no record at all of this; furthermore his style does not reflect the 'Cox influence' like Ince's.

Further to Ince's knowledge of what was under the water of the rivers, he would have watched the dipper bobbing, the flash of the iridescent king-fisher, the elegance of the grey wagtail and heard, across the marshy banks in summer the curlew giving its warbling, fluty call. He would have known in autumn when they left, high up in the sky, for their winters at the coasts, giving their eerie whistle in the clouds. The cry of the lapwings he would have mimicked, 'pee-wit!' and, been highly delighted if, walking back and forth he had found those near invisible stone coloured eggs, splotched in black. Where the winter floods had created red earth mini cliffs he noticed tiny sand martins hawking for midges and may flies over the water, and speeding into their colony of holes. He knew otters and water voles; water shrews, and, higher up the banks, badgers and foxes, and hedgehogs in the alder holts. In short, he was a country boy, with a great awareness and love of the miracles around him. All farming in those times was organic, and in

13

the summer he could play in meadows of permanent pasture, full of the natural, and beautiful different grasses which smell so sweet: cocksfoot, timothy, meadow fescue, Yorkshire fog — soft and pink, quaking grass, and clovers white and red where the petals could be pulled out and the nectar sipped. Also cornflower, yellow Welsh poppies, buttercups, cowslips and oxlips. The springs running down to the Lugg both sides of Presteigne created patches of watermeadow which never dried out, and had their own special plants, such as marsh marigold and water plantain. Butterflies were everywhere, many cottages kept skeps (straw hives) for honey bees, and boys were told firmly never to interfere or throw stones at a wasp's or hornet's nest! Every year the clog makers would appear from the north of England working in the Withy Beds and making their wooden clogs from the alders.

One of the highlights of the summer was a full scale picnic. Several families loaded up their traps and wagonettes and together they would toil up the hill past Rowley and Beggar's Bush, thence on to New Radnor and park the vehicles and the horses somewhere along the valley below the Mynd. The sense of mystery started here, for there were even black rabbits to be seen! Some took the higher part to cross, and look down, on Water-Break-Its-Neck, others would walk up the brook itself, and gaze up at the falls, the boys certainly daring each other to climb the mossy, slippery sides. It was an echoing, magic place; a larch grove grew near the top, silencing footballs with its carpet of fine needles, nothing but the soft sighing of the wind in the feathery branches. After a picnic lunch, veal and ham pie, maybe chicken, a pressed tongue and slices of brawn, the young ones would explore still further up, finding Llewellyn's Cave and scrambling up through the heather of Esgerantau.

This steep dingle of Water-Break-Its-Neck, covered with many exotic ferns, including the six foot high Osmunda or Royal Fern, (which was pillaged by the plant hunting Victorians), inspired the young artist to paint it twice, and to make a lithograph for his *Seven Views of Radnorshire* many years later.

Winter would have brought its own excitements. Winters were then much harsher and skating was eagerly anticipated, being particularly good when floods came first and then froze, so that wide areas of comparatively shallow and safe waters were made into racing areas. Boys with no skates had long 'slides'. In order to 'grip' and be able to be driven on packed snow in safety, horses had their shoes removed, or special nails used so that the snow did not 'pack up'. Some of the burghers would have had sleighs that could bowl along quite fast with two passengers, a groom on the humble seat at the rear helping the balance, with most sleighs being fitted with bells, it was a real Christmas sound indeed![3]

Shooting was not the pastime of great organised syndicates as it is now. A few farmers would get together with their spaniels and retrievers and 'walk up some land'. A favourite dog then was the 'pointer', freezing, motionless and unerringly showing there was game ahead. The gun used was a still a muzzle loader and a very heavy weapon, with its accompanying powdering flask of brass or copper, now a collector's find.

Fox hunting was with private trencher fed packs, the start of the Radnor and West only came later. There was a pack kept at Llanfihangel Nant Melyn and one at Kington. Winter, too, meant parties, and Joseph would not have been very old when he was taught dancing.

One thing only interfered with this idyllic life, it went by the name of school!

Dr. Ince must have known that the local Grammar School — the second oldest independent one in Wales, was going through a 'low' period. It would have been much commented upon by the worthies of the town and his son Henry had been there for six or seven years before Ince minor was considered ready to start his education.

The reasons for the decline had started long before; in 1565 John Beddoes, the founder, a wealthy woollen manufacturer, or clothier, as it was termed in the reign of Queen Elizabeth I, had endowed the school very carefully. As a result of the terms in his Deed of Feoffment, he had caused the school to be described as one of the wealthiest in Wales. However, there was a gap in the legal arrangements; this was that new trustees should have been appointed as soon as vacancies had arisen, as occurred through death.

Over the course of the next 250 years the number of trustees been allowed to fall below the permitted minimum of three (with the inevitable difficulty of appointing new ones), nor had appointments which had been made been vetted for their suitability, and it had become more of a 'nominal' distinction to be a trustee, with certain individuals having no intention of fulfilling their duty towards the school. Indeed, in 1821 when a new headmaster was required, it was found that the school lands had actually passed into the estate of the last of the trustees to have died without anyone in Presteigne knowing! It had become necessary for the Court of Chancery to step in, in order that nine other trustees could be appointed.

While Ince was at school, the Head was the Reverend John Grubb, whose time with the school can only be viewed with, at least, suspicion due to the rumoured misappropriation of funds. He was vicar of Wigmore and a magistrate, and presumably he received the rents of the lands belonging to the school. Ince in fact was lucky, because just as he was leaving Robert Phillips was elected headmaster who had been running a school at the Red House in Broad Street on the lines of Dotheboys Hall in Dickens' *Nicholas Nickleby*! According to his advertisement for this nefarious establishment 'Young gentlemen are genteelly boarded, no entrance is charged, nor will there be any vacations'. It is interesting that a few years later he was deemed by the Welsh Education Commission as being 'in body and mind utterly unfit for his post'.

In the past, John Beddoes School had claim to at least a dozen Oxford University Exhibitions or Scholarships. Latin had been a must, and most pupils could read and write Latin as fluently as they did English. Dr. Ince would probably have seen to it that his sons had some extra tuition in both Greek and Latin from the Rector, the Reverend James Beebee.

The original school had been in St. David's Street, but had been destroyed by the great fire of 12 September 1681. During Ince's time it was located next to Garrison House, by the churchyard, in which lived the headmaster and a few boarders. It was an easy walk for young Ince from Broad Street. There were about 50 pupils, all boys. The school day started with breakfast at 7:30am, dinner was at 11, lessons continuing until 5pm. There was a half

Ince's sketch of men scything[4]

holiday once a week, usually on Saturday. Church on Sunday was a must for the boarders. Holidays were Christmas, Easter and at harvest time (at which most boys would help). Church feasts (such as Ascension Day and St. Andrew's Day) were also observed as holidays, as was Presteigne's Midsummer Fair, instituted in the 13th century, and the 12 May Hiring Fair.

When the school was first founded, it had been imperative that boys were skilled in the use of the bow. For instance, at Ruthin Grammar School (founded in 1574) a document exists in which parents are told 'Ye shall allow your child at all times a bow, three shafts at least, bow strings, a bracer and shooting glove to exercise shooting'. A game like rounders was played, and a rough kind of football — there was also wrestling and boxing (but not as we know it!). For the playground, there was fives, various traditional games, even conkers!

It is doubtful that Ince went to Preparatory school, although there was one in Lyonshall advertising itself 'for reception of young gentlemen from 3 to 8 years old preparatory to Grammar school'. It would have been too far to go daily in winter, and it is much more likely he would have had early lessons privately with a tutor or retired school master living in the town; sometimes neighbouring families would share a governess, and there were several around Presteigne with responsibility for many children.

John Beddoes and his school are also entwined with Presteigne's curfew bell. He had stipulated that a 'day bell' should be rung for ever from the parish church — for half-an-hour from 6am in the winter and 5am in the summer. The curfew bell was also to be rung for ever, at 8pm in the evening, winter and summer, again for half-an-hour. The day bell became a useful alarm clock for everyone and, on winters' nights in terrible snowstorms, the curfew bell had saved lives, guiding people who were lost towards the town. Beddoes had set out in the Deed of Uses for the school that if the running of the curfew bell was not adhered to, then the endowment, school and all associated lands should revert to the heirs of John Beddoes. To this day it is rung, though not for half an hour; the only break in history has been either through plague or during the Second World War.

All pupils hoped it would be school holiday time when the drovers were on their way over from Wales. News of their arrival would have been received with great excitement by the boys of Presteigne and they would certainly have walked or ridden their ponies into the hills around promising anxious mothers to come back. The noise of the drovers calling to their stock, a cross between a hunting 'holloa', yodelling, and sheep dog whistling, could by all accounts be heard miles away. 'Droving', taking the wild and beautiful Welsh Blacks to the richer lowland pastures of England had been going on for many hundreds of years, long even before the middle ages. The roast beef of Old England owes its reputation to the black cattle of Wales.

A man could apply for a droving licence if he was over 30, married and a householder and would then hire his men, their wages being higher than those for a farm labourer. It was also the custom for anyone wishing to go to London or to the East of England to ride with the drovers. The pace may only have been two miles an hour, but there was security in the company of the drovers, and young men of quality would often ride along too (with their own pistols). In many places they would be able to stop at inns. Cattle had to be shod with the famous 'cues', two pieces to fit the cloven hoof. Even pigs had little boots when they were droved. A well known shoeing forge was at Cregrina. The 'latest' news the drovers brought back with them was always eagerly sought after. (Imagine coming back with the news of Waterloo). Added to this they would often be entrusted with commissions, maybe to buy material for a lady, or to pay an allowance to a rich man's son studying in the city. With the money they were given to carry, and received, from the sale of stock, robberies were inevitable and it is for this reason the banks were formed. The Bank of the Black Horse started as the Bank of the Black Ox. Again, we can see from Ince's paintings of the hills and his treatment of horses and dogs, how well he observed the animals around him and his knowledge of their anatomy is remarkable for the time.

A series of sketches made by Ince on the theme of milking (notice the Welsh hats)

A sketch made by Ince of the lane leading towards Stapleton Castle
which is shown on its hill to the right (National Library of Wales)

At school, young Ince would have had a wider circle of friends, with boys coming in from neighbouring farms and they would certainly have told him, with ghoulish embellishments, of the folk tales and ghost stories that abounded. Of the 'Lady Bluefoot' of Stapleton Castle — and dared him to pass at twilight that place of 'murder most foul', while they would chant 'Lady Bluefoot, all in black. Silver buttons down her back. Harigoshee! Harigoshee! Lock the cupboard and take the key'. There was indeed, a horrible legend recounted of this place, a tale of a villainous Reeve left in charge while his Knight had gone to the Crusades. He told the lady of the castle that her husband had died, had the young heir kidnapped, and then tried to marry the lady. When she refused, he murdered her and hid her body.

However a much happier, albeit later, tale is recounted from Chancery Proceedings, 1335:[5] 'Geoffrey Cornewall born at Stapleton Castle in 1335, baptised St Andrews. William de la Mere remembered the day because he was Squire to Dame Margaret (née de Mortimer, Grandmother of the Infant) who sent him to the Abbot of Wigmore to pray the same to be god father. The babe was carried back from the church to Stapleton with chanting and a great escort of many praising God for the birth of the aforesaid Geoffrey.' In 1365 the said Geoffrey was succeeded by his son Bryan — hence we have Bryan's Ground in Letchmoor Lane. Sir John Cornewall married Elizabeth, Henry IV's sister and it is recorded that the king did come to visit his sister here twice. Sir John took 30 men at arms and 90 Welsh archers to Agincourt. For several hundred years there were many trophies of that battle held at Stapleton Castle.

There were many other supernatural tales, of a ghost at Monaughty of a sad lady, of King Charles I's horses that could be heard at night coming from Walton and Beggar's Bush, of St. Anne who sat by her holy well in Brink Lane, bathing the eyes of blind beggars, of the Roman soldiers who stood guard at Corton, caring for the silver votive offerings to the Goddess of the Spring there, (found many years later in 1940). There was a highwayman, Dick Green, arrested at Greenfield House and hung in Gallows Lane, as many other felons had been; the gibbet creaked at night, and Gallows Lane was to be avoided. One cannot imagine now that a journey in the dark from Kington to Presteigne could have been hazardous and frightening. Yet, for instance, my grandmother, driving the pony and trap in the dusk, past the marshes at Bullocks Mill would say to the children 'don't look, cover your eyes, cover your eyes' that they might not see the Will o' the Wisp who could lure them away to their deaths.

No greater fear was there than that of Black Vaughan of Hergest. Presteigne had an affinity with this legend of evil because it had been in Presteigne Church that the exorcism of Black Vaughan's spirit had taken place. The basic tale of the curse of the Vaughans of Hergest seems to have been started about 1400. Hergest was a fortified stronghold then, with, according to Lewis Glyn Cothi, the Bard, 'eight towers'. It was a place of much feasting, Bardic music and poetry. It had certainly not been unusual for the 'Lord of the Manor' to take a girl who caught his eye and keep her by force until his ardour waned. In this case, however, the lass must have had tremendous spirit. During the feasting, she escaped down the ivy from an upstairs room and fled. It would have made sense that she would not have gone to her father's house in Kington, for it would have been searched and the family probably killed. So she climbed over Hergest Ridge and down the other side and across to Stanner Rocks, where in all probability she would have hoped to find a cave to conceal herself.

Vaughan, finding himself tricked and in a furious and drunken rage shouted for his horse and his hounds. (In those days they would have been

Kington church as sketched by Ince

akin to Irish Wolfhounds crossed with Mastiffs). Here he swore, in front of his guests, the oath that was his undoing. 'If I do not get her the Devil can take my Soul'. Suddenly, among his hounds his friends saw, with growing horror, a huge black hound they had never seen before. After the hounds had picked up the scent and were over the brow of Hergest towards Stanner, a riderless horse came galloping back to the followers, Vaughan's horse, and they could hear hounds whimpering in a cowed and frightened way. When they reached the top of the rocks they saw Vaughan's body below and that of the girl, but standing over the man was this ghastly black hound tearing his throat out! From that moment on, Kington lived with sightings at night, both of this hound and of Black Vaughan and there was very real fear. There were even recorded deaths by heart failure of people who had seen the spectre.

The fear was there even four hundred years later. W.S. Symonds the Rector of Pendock, wrote *Malvern Chase* in 1881 with a frightening account of 'The Hound of Hergest'. It would be fair to assume that Arthur Conan Doyle with his interest in the occult, certainly read it and he had stayed in Kington for a time. My father, a solicitor in London, was also keenly interested, (in fact he took several statements from those who swore they had witnessed this horror). He discussed this with Sir Arthur. I hold a letter, hand written and signed by the latter which states that his book *The Hound of the Baskervilles* is just based on a 'West Country Legend'. This was on the advice of my father, who had warned him to cover himself from possible litigation from the family. Soon after, the direct line of the Vaughans of Hergest died out. The Baskervilles had given Conan Doyle permission to use their name, whilst local names such as Mortimer and Stapleton are given to characters in the book. To place the story on Dartmoor was a

The marriage certificate of Henry Griffiths, Henry Ince's illegitimate son

wise decision, after all there are phantom hounds all over the country!

Ince would have known also about Silver John, the beloved bone setter and healer who was murdered for his silver buttons, as he would never take payment in money. When the weather was cold enough at Candlemas Fair to skate on Llynhyllen pool he would, with other boys, ghoulishly recount how Silver John's body was discovered under the ice. But good Silver John never haunted anyone, and his body was laid to rest up the Harley Valley under the Great Cregiau.

The trial of Mary Morgan was too recent in Presteigne to have assumed legendary status. It was still a guilty memory for those living and therefore not mentioned.

There are not many paintings by Ince influenced by legend unless the one of Stapleton Castle, interesting because it was still inhabited, inspired him for reasons over and above its beautiful setting. There is also his light hearted *Jack in the Green* (plate 13), which seems to have been a spring time frolic in which the Green Man is involved. This picture was probably painted in much later life, when he was living in Cambridge.

Plates 1 to 11 (this and next 3 pages). Illustrations by Ince
when it is thought he was aged 13 to 14. These sketches show clearly Ince's
talent for showing texture — whether in copper, glass, saltware or wicker

While at school, Ince painted when and where he could, even in the kitchen, and his notebook, now held in Hereford Museum, is a little masterpiece. Here he shows his genius for texture. The winking copperware, the surface of the salt glazed pots, the pliable basket ware; this ability is amazing at the age of 14 and we have a Vermeer touch in giving ordinary humble every day objects a life of their own (see plates 1-11).

In the meantime, Dr. Ince would have been looking for a way to channel his older son's energies in the small town of Presteigne, but not entirely successfully it appears. Young Henry may have spent time at John Beddoes Free Grammar School or have been sent to Hereford, but whether he benefited from the experience is questionable. Dr. Ince clearly decided that a spell of military experience would be beneficial for his son and enrolled him in the Royal Berkshire Militia, his own first regiment, the regimental records showing that Henry Ince was commissioned as ensign on 21 December 1815,[6] shortly after his 18th birthday. Presumably his father reasoned that there was little risk of his son being killed in the line of duty. The battle of Waterloo had been fought and won in June 1815 and disarmament was the order of the day. The Berkshire Militia had been in Ireland to prevent any rising by the Irish Catholics, but it had returned to Liverpool and then marched back to Reading during October and November 1815. Henry Ince must have joined the regiment in Reading but never saw active service. The end of the Napoleonic War meant that the expense of keeping men under arms had to be reduced as rapidly as possible and on 14 March 1816, the Berkshire Militia was put into mothballs.

The commissioned staff remained in post (and continued to be paid) but there were no men to command and no duties to carry out, except for occasional training exercises. No doubt Henry Ince looked splendid in his uniform and must have cut a dash when he returned to Presteigne, presumably to live at home with his parents and brother. He certainly seems to have had success with the ladies, or with one at least, although her identity is uncertain. The marriage register of the parish church of Bleddfa records that on 2 October 1838 Henry Griffiths, aged 21, a shoemaker, married Nancy Mitton, aged 23, a farmer's daughter. The register further records that the father of Henry Griffiths was a Henry Ince. The only known Inces in Radnorshire in 1817, the year of Henry Griffiths's birth, were the family of Dr. Henry Ince. The most likely father of the illegitimate baby is young Henry Ince, returned from his military service and with time on his hands.

The Ince family cared for the child and saw to it that he learned a trade. It is likely that Henry Griffiths was apprenticed to a shoemaker and that he lodged with his master, all paid for by Dr. Ince. The choice of trade is significant; in due course, two of Henry Ince's legitimate offspring were apprenticed as shoemakers. Henry and Nancy Griffiths can be traced through the census records, with Henry Griffiths plying his trade and raising a family in the border country. There were four children. Matilda was born in 1843 in Leintwardine; Elizabeth (1850) and Albert (1852) were born in Knighton, before the family returned to Leintwardine where Joseph Andrew was born in 1857. The family were still in Swan Street, Leintwardine in 1861, when Henry described himself as a 'shoemaker (master)'. By 1871 the family had moved to Smethwick near Birmingham when Henry Griffiths and his son, Albert, were both recorded as bootmakers. Henry must have made a success of his career because the 1881 census records that a Henry Griffiths, widower aged 63, was now a retired shoemaker. At the time of the census, he was visiting his daughter, now Matilda Gregory, and his grandchildren in Southport, Lancashire.

A sense of the society in which Ince grew up can be ascertained by considering the families living in and around Presteigne during the first half of the nineteenth century, some of his neighbours becoming life-long friends in due course.

The Meyrick family's[7] home and business was the butchers' shop on the corner of the High Street, looking down Broad Street, a half-timbered house — Jacobean and over hung. There were 12 children of the marriage between Thomas King Meyrick and Cassandra Stanton. Edward Stanton Meyrick (incidentally my great grandfather) was the closest in age to Ince, being born in 1804. They both went to

This portrait of Thomas King Meyrick was painted by William J. Chapman in 1842. A copy of the painting existed as a fresco on the back wall of the butcher's shop, but is now covered over

Edward Stanton Meyrick

London in 1826 and lived in the same district. Edward became an importer of wines and, like Ince, would return to Presteigne every year. He too was a keen fisherman.

Another Presteigne family of the period were the Barneses. James Barnes was born in 1788 near Barnet and like his father was commissioned in the Royal Horse Guards — The Blues. (His father had been quarter-master of the regiment and died at Windsor in the 50th year of his service.) James fought under Wellington in the Peninsular Wars and earned the General Service Medal 1703–1814 with clasps for Vittoria and Toulouse. In 1819, aged only 25, he sold his commission and moved to Presteigne where he bought a house in Broad Street. By owning property he was qualified to become a JP and duly purchased other property in Stapleton and Presteigne with large acreages. He was a colourful retired soldier for the boys to talk to. He was also a visiting magistrate to the gaol and in 1825 he re-captured two escapees who had overpowered the warders! With his former war experience, in 1823 he was appointed Captain in the Royal Radnorshire Militia. He had five children and they certainly lived their early life in Broad Street, but by 1846 he had moved to Caledon, 60 or 70 miles east of Cape Town. The younger sons did not follow

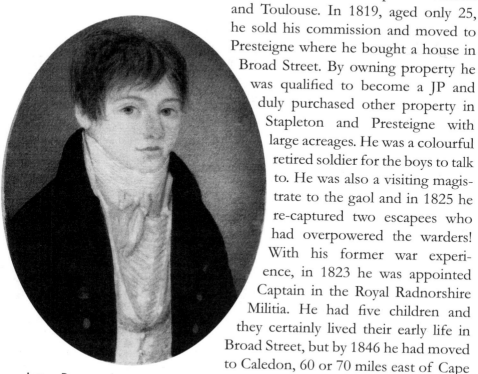

James Barnes when a young man

him until later and from the Barnes family records we find that Edward Robert Bigsby Barnes had painting lessons from Ince in Presteigne, this young boy benefited from his tuition and became a good painter, some of his paintings are now in Florida. However at the same time that James Barnes lived in Presteigne, a famous kinsman of his lived in Portishead, Bristol, his name was Lieutenant General Sir Edward Barnes G.C.B. and visits from this family would have been quite an event in Presteigne. He had led a brigade at Vittoria, was wounded at Waterloo, and became Governor of Ceylon in 1824–1831 during which time he directed the construction of the Great Military Road between Colombo and Kandy. Later in 1831 he was appointed Commander in Chief in India. When he returned home he became MP for Sudbury in 1837.[8]

Another warrior who lived in Presteigne for a while when not at sea was Admiral Sir Peter Puget. The Pugets came over when the Huguenots were being persecuted by Louis XIV and settled in London, founding the Bank of Puget and Bainbridge which by 1784 had become London agents for the Bank of Ireland. Peter's older brother eventually became a director to the Bank of England.

Peter however, joined the Navy as a midshipman in 1778 (still not quite 13!) and sailed to the West Indies and then Gibraltar. He soon became a second officer, serving under Captain Roberts in *HMS Discovery*. She had been sent to the west coast of North America under the overall command of Captain Vancouver. They were surveying that part of the coast 30° to 60° north searching for the northwest passage, (hopefully to circumnavigate the world). Puget proved himself a first class surveyor and in 1793 was put in command of *HMS Chatham*, an armed tender. By 1797 he had risen to the rank of captain and over the next seven years commanded several ships. In 1804–5 he took part in the blockade of the French fleet in Brest harbour in command of the *Foudroyant*. By 1807 he was engaged in Copenhagen and by 1809 in the Baltic, and was then appointed commissioner for the navy in Madras in 1810–1818. In 1819 he was gazetted as Knight Commander of the Order of the Bath and in 1821, through seniority, became Rear Admiral of the Blue.

He had married Hannah Elrington and in 1801 moved to Presteigne with his young family of three sons; he had six more children by 1812. They lived firstly at Broadheath House, but in 1807 they moved to the Red House in Broad Street. Hannah's father was an army man — a Lieutenant and Quartermaster — stationed in Hereford, so she had family near while her husband was at sea. Puget had an old friend, Captain Joseph Baker, who had risen from third officer in the *Discovery* to finally take command and who came to live in St. David's Street. Captain Baker was a great draughtsman and had drawn many charts of the sounds and channels around Vancouver; Baker Island in the Columbia river and Mount Baker in Washington were named after him. When Puget bought the Red House in 1806, Baker acted as his agent and Puget's fifth child was christened Joseph Baker after him. (Joseph Baker's memorial tablet is in the Lady Chapel, St. Andrew's Church, Presteigne). Not to be outdone by Baker, Admiral Sir Peter Puget had Puget Island in the Columbia river named after him, Cape Puget in Alaska and Puget Sound between Vancouver Island and Washington state on the west coast. How the children must have loved to listen to the tales of adventure and exploration. The admiral became a trustee of the Radnorshire Turnpike Trust and a JP. However when he returned shore side at last, the family went back to live in London and finally to Bath. He died in October 1822 of the gout.

The Lewis family had lived for over 300 years at Harpton Court and many of them are buried in Old Radnor Church. A document in Brampton Bryan tells us of an 'affray' that took place on 2 October 1693 in the streets of Old Radnor, swords being drawn on both sides. Thomas Lewis aided by his brother Nourse was described as the aggressor, and his antagonist was a Harley of Brampton Bryan.

A Gloucestershire paper reports in September 1724 that there died at Bath Thomas Lewis of Harpton Court, Radnorshire: 'Father to the representative in Parliament for the Borough of New Radnor, his corpse was met on the road by near 700 horsemen of whom very much bewailed the loss of him who was a favourite of the rich, a father of the poor, a most judicious Magistrate of the Court'. He and his wife Margaret had eight children, one of whom, Isabella, married a cousin, John Lewis of Presteigne. Their sons Robert and John founded a timber yard there, ran a tannery and were maltsters as well. In the portrait we can see timber in the landscape background. Robert lived in Broad Street and brought up his niece, Anne-Harriet, presumably because her father, John, lived in a very isolated part of the country near Monmouth, from where he managed part of the family's business in Monmouth and London. When the new Judge's Lodgings were completed in 1823 it always fell on one of the good citizens of Presteigne to entertain the Judge to lunch while he was here for the Assizes. A letter written by a great aunt of mine refers to such an occasion

Robert Lewis, a timber merchant, who lived in Broad Street

and is rather endearing. 'I remember Grannie telling me that her uncle was entertaining the Judge at the Law Courts for lunch. The Judge had disrobed while at lunch and his gown and wig were in the hall and Grannie who was only a little girl at the time, put on the wig and gown and was caught! I cannot remember the punishment!'

Then there was the Galliers family, of Norman descent as their name suggests, who had been farmers for generations. They were the last family who actually lived at Stapleton Castle, 'reformed' as a house after the Civil War in which it had been slighted on the orders of Cromwell, using many of the old stones and some of the timbers. They were noted breeders of cattle, favouring their own 'mottle faced' but eventually coming round to the white faced reds — the Herefords. John Galliers stayed at the Castle with his parents, marrying Charlotte by whom he had a son, another John, exactly the same age as Joseph Murray Ince. In 1808 Mary-Ann was born, followed by Thomas and then Eliza in 1814. William Galliers, John senior's brother, lived in Broad Street at Brook House and he's noted in the parish registers as 'Land Surveyor'. He became well known for the most beautiful maps (one of which can be seen in Leominster museum), and he was commissioned by James King, late of the East India Company and owner of Stanton Park, to map the whole estate. James King died in 1822 and it was 1843 before another James inherited who doubled the name and was called King-King.

In E. Heath Agnew's *A History of Hereford Cattle*, it is noted James Turner started breeding Hereford Cattle at Aymestrey Court before 1780. Here he 'founded the herd which probably exerted more influence through its female lines than any other in the history of the breed'. James' four sons continued the breeding. Phillip stayed at Aymestrey Court and then moved to West Court, John was at Court of Noke on the edge of Staunton-on-Arrow, Samuel Downes Turner went to Lynch Court, and Thomas to found the Arrow Lodge Mills and to farm at Kington. Phillip's son, another Phillip, went to the Leen near Pembridge where on his death, his son Arthur took over. Quite a dynasty! How could anyone have seen at the beginning that within 30 years 'the gentle giants with white faces' would have made the name Hereford known all over the world. The Argentine, USA, Canada, Australia and Uruguay were clamouring for the stock which stood up to any climate, even drought, and had a natural immunity to T.B. The Hereford Herd Book Society was registered in 1816 and by this time, many well known names were breeders.

At the Rodd,[9] Aaron Rogers had married Harriet Lewis, daughter of John Lewis of Presteigne whom we have already mentioned. The Rogers family became great breeders of Hereford cattle as later we see in an epic poem which was written in 1889 (30 years after Joseph Murray Ince's death) and called *The American buyer's directory of pedigree Herefords*. Ben Rogers (Aaron's uncle) had bred the great bull 'Sir Benjamin' at the Grove in Pembridge and Aaron himself bred 'Sir Archibald' both exported for what were then enormous sums to the Argentine.

The Stephens were an old and respected family going back many generations to the Stephens of Castle Vale of Llannano who were High Sheriffs in 1689 — when Roger Stephens of Knowle held the office. In 1710 Elizabeth Lewis of Harpton married the son, also Roger Stephens, but of Barland, between Presteigne and Evenjobb. Moving ahead to the time when Ince was young, there was Thomas and Ann Stephens of The Broadheath with a son William, and another family of Stephens living at Green End. Nearly all the Stephens were solicitors and appeared to own quite big estates in the parishes of Presteigne and Glascwm. Several of the Stephens intermarried with many of the Presteigne dynasties.[10]

Cecil Parsons, who became a close friend of Dr. Ince, was a solicitor who lived at Bridge House, a substantial house in Presteigne by the river Lugg. He became an eminent lawyer and Deputy Lieutenant of Radnorshire. There is no record of his marriage on his memorial in the church, but he had four brothers who died whilst in the army, two in the Peninsular campaign. He himself died in 1876 aged 90.

Nowdays it would seem excessive, but in 1807 when Dr. Ince arrived in Presteigne, there were three doctors, but we have already considered the

Ince's sketch of Presteigne from the banks of the Lugg.
Note that the church tower had a cupola then

distances that they had to cover. By 1835 indeed there are four doctors listed in Pigot's *Directory*: Vincent Cooksey in the High Street, Aaron Davies MD in St. David's Street, Henry Robert Ince surgeon in St David's Street and Edward Meredith in Hereford Street. In Pigot's 1830 *Directory* the name 'Ince and Cross' is listed for St. David's Street at an address also given as Dr. Ince's place of abode, so it must be assumed that he was then in part-nership. The house now known as Warden Court was rebuilt at this time and it does seem that it was used as a surgery, with a side entrance onto St. David's Street. Besides having an ample coach house and stabling it was wonderfully central for the town. When Joseph Murray Ince was subse-quently resident in the town in his own right, he always lived at Roseland in Broad Street, but his mother, Anne Elizabeth, had died in 1830 and it was possibly more convenient thereafter for Dr. Ince to live at the surgery. It is a large house and would have easily accommodated two resident doctors. In 1847 Warden Court was bought by W. Stephens, solicitor and clerk of the peace.

A feel for the area around Presteigne at the time is given in Byron's letters and journals.[11] Byron enjoyed staying in these parts to be near the beautiful Lady Harley, the wife of the Earl of Oxford at Eywood, Titley, who was so notoriously unfaithful that the children were known as the Harleian Miscellanae. On 24th October 1812 Byron wrote to Lady Melbourne 'I'm just setting off, detestable roads – [Eywood].' Six days later, again talking of Eywood he notes: 'The country round this place is wild and consequently very delightful.' Just a few days later he wrote: 'This country is very to my taste and I have taken a seat of Lord Oxford's (Kinsham Court, about 5 miles off) in a delightful situation, for next year.'

3   The Young Artist

An account in the *Hereford Journal* for 5 June 1816 says that: 'amongst the premiums distributed on Friday last at Freemason Tavern by his Royal Highness the Duke of Sussex, President of the Society for the encouragement of the Arts etc., it was with pleasure we observe the name of Master John Scarlet (*sic*) Davis, a young, self taught genius, 11 years of age, from the borough of Leominster, and son of James Davis, as a successful candidate in Anatomical engravings.' It was also noted that the duke, on presenting Davis with the Silver Palette prize, remarked that he was so much younger (and smaller) than any of the other candidates, he did not immediately see him!

The Marquis of Stafford and several other influential members of the Society were present, and there is no doubt the boy was noticed. Davis remained at school in Leominster for another two years, during which time he made numerous portraits and sketches of the locals, usually selling them for £1 each. He was brilliant at portraiture and, later in his career, in the study of buildings and architecture. Ince and John Scarlett Davis became friends early on and remained so all their lives, as we shall see.

With Scarlett Davis' success in obtaining entry to de la Pierre's, Dr. Ince must have started to seriously think of his own son's future training. How fortunate then, that the timing fitted so perfectly — that David Cox (already starting to attain, if not fame, certainly the hint of it) was living in Hereford and was available to take on resident pupils. Dr. Ince paid 70 guineas a year for Ince's tuition and keep for three years, then no mean sum.

David Cox was the son of a blacksmith, born near Birmingham at Deritend, then a village for the Industrial Revolution had not yet overtaken the Midlands. David had great pride in the skill and precision of his father's profession and even later in his life he would examine the bayonets of soldiers in the London parks to find either his father's trademark or his initials on a horseshoe. They were a loving family and, when famous, David never forgot them, always paying an annuity to his father. The story goes that young David tripped over a door scraper one dark night and broke his leg. Thus a normally active little boy was restricted for weeks on end by the healing process, during which cousin, Allport, gave him a box of colours. He would paint and copy anything from prints to children's kites, and his parents, seeing that friends actually <u>paid</u> for his work, managed to get him to a night school for drawing, run by Joseph Barber who was a strong disciplinarian in matters of art.

He was apprenticed in 1775 to John Taylor, a manufacturer of hand painted and enamelled buckles and snuff boxes. In truth, this was speed painting, but it did cross over to miniature work for some clients desired a more personal and individual memento. This led to David being re-apprenticed to a locket and miniature painter called Fielder. However, a dreadful incident occurred. One morning, arriving for work, Cox found Fielder had hung himself. The suicide was a terrible shock and could have badly disturbed the boy for some time, but his cousin Allport again stepped in, and found him a job as a colour grinder and general help in the scene painting department of the Birmingham Theatre. From painting miniatures to wielding big brushes on backdrops was a contrast indeed — but it opened his eyes to the broad effect. The chief scene painter was James de Maria, of great reputation; not only had he come from the Opera House in London but knew J.M.W. Turner well, and had accompanied the latter on some of his painting tours. De Maria's famous panorama of Paris in 1802 had been compared in style to the painting of the Welsh artist Richard Wilson. The clever illusion incorporated in stage paintings was not taken up by Cox in later life, but in his generous fashion, he never underestimated this important part of his career and meeting De Maria much later, he was able to tell him how much his influence had meant. In like generous frame, the elderly De Maria acknowledged the benefits had been mutual and that the student had become himself a master.

In 1804, having turned down an offer from a travelling circus company to paint scenery, Cox went to London, determined to make his name as a freelance painter. He found lodgings which turned out to be not only comfortable, but led to a wonderful stroke of fate. It is almost a music hall joke 'marrying the landlady's daughter', but how fortunate it was for him. David was quiet and too self effacing, but Mary Ragg, 12 years his senior was an educated and discerning woman. She taught him to read and would herself read to him as he painted. He sold his early paintings very cheaply, but at least the income covered their living expenses. He subscribed to the *Liber Studiorum* by J.M.W. Turner (a series showing different kinds of landscapes as engravings published between 1806 and 1819), which gave David his great admiration for Turner. This search to learn made him take lessons from Varley, a friend of William Blake and a fellow astrologer. Realising Cox was a professional artist and admiring his humility and sincerity, Varley waived the fee and allowed Cox to watch him as he worked. Cox had two paintings hung in the Academy in 1805: *Kenilworth Castle* and *A View of the River Mersey*. After this he preferred to exhibit with the new, and very successful, Society of Artists in Watercolour. However it was teaching that provided the necessary income. This was the era when every young lady of quality had to paint as part of her education, and Cox's pupils included many titled aspirants who had been introduced to him by the heir of the Earl of Plymouth, Colonel the Hon. Henry Windsor, who was himself a keen student. Even then it was only after the insistence of the Colonel's mother that Cox raised the cost of his lessons to 10 shillings and 6 pence.

It seems strange to think that it was so difficult to make a living when it was such a fashionable time for lessons. But Cox was a true artist, his heart was never in teaching, which was why, in 1813, he published his *Treatise on Landscape Painting and Effect in Watercolours* at the urgent request of his pupils. It is as relevant today as it was then. He insisted on 'a proper feeling for the subject', and that 'a picture should be complete and perfect in the mind before it is put upon the canvas'. He made a special emphasis on tonal values — and above all the importance of the line as the structure and the skeleton of the painting.

Later in 1813 he was offered and took the post of drawing master at the Military College at Farnham, Surrey, where he was given the rank of Captain and of course a batman. Indeed, he quite enjoyed the social side, but his work was exacting and needed great precision in the drawing of maps and truly this did not interest him, so after a year or so he resigned.

It was then that he saw the advertisement in *The Times* by Miss Croucher offering £100 a year for teaching twice a week in her school for young ladies in Widemarsh Street, Hereford. He and his wife saw that this would give him not only the freedom to paint for himself, but to take pupils of his own as well and would bring him nearer to his beloved Wales. This was everything to the man who loved the countryside so intensely that his friends often called him 'Farmer Cox'.

The cottage in Parry Lane, Hereford, where Cox lived for six and a half years

After renting a very basic cottage at Lower Lyde, near Aylestone Hill, his first winter must have been a trial, but in 1815 he moved to George Cottage near Baynton Wood. Then in 1817 he found a pleasant cottage in Parry Lane and an understanding landlord who allowed him to build on a studio. He stayed there, in Parry Lane, for six and a half years. The support and business sense of his wife Mary was very evident during this time, for Cox bought a plot on Aylestone Hill and built Ash Tree House, which he sold on well in 1827.

Cox, as usual, hated the drudge (to him) of teaching, he was also giving classes at the Grammar school and a private school run by a Miss Poole. He had some outlying pupils too. Sadly, the army had not taught him to ride, so although he bought a pony to carry him around the countryside, it was not a success, and after a couple of falls he gave up that idea, preferring to walk.

He loved gardening all his life and in Hereford he would grow his favourite hollyhocks and other broad-leafed plants that feature in many of his landscapes.

Cox's style was now becoming a little more precise, although his washes and tones remained as individual and free as ever and he did not become topographical as the times demanded (it was very fashionable then to have one's own house painted in landscape setting). He also published *Progressive Lessons in Landscape for Young Beginners* illustrated with some of his etchings. He would have had good sales as his many pupils would have bought a copy. He also found time to make *Six Views of Bath* aquatinted by S. & J. Fuller. When Ince went to him as a student it must have been a happy time for him; Cox's courtesy and his honesty was a byword and never changed. The household was well run by Mrs. Cox; and there was young David Cox, who was 14 years old by 1823. The only other resident pupil then was the son of the Duke of Beaufort's agent. Mrs. Cox had a devoted servant, Ann Fowler, who had already been with them for some years and remained on as housekeeper and faithful retainer with David Cox after his wife had died. Painting excursions would have been made from Hereford into Wales and down the Wye, for Cox always liked to have companions with him. Excursions to the theatre would have been an attraction too.

Advertisements for theatre performances that Cox might have enjoyed attending

It was truly fortunate for Ince that he had the guiding hand and inspiration of David Cox for, to use a modern phrase, they were both 'on the same wavelength'. Ince did not have to spend days and weeks drawing classical statues or making meticulous copies of Claude or Wilson. Ince went to London in 1826, followed later by the Cox family. Cox's position was gradually becoming more secure and through him Ince must have got to know Samuel Prout, John Sell Cotman, John Crome, Samuel Palmer and John Linell. Cox also knew J.M.W. Turner who was very fond of him, always mysteriously referring to him as Daniel, and who gave him a painting.

In 1826 Cox travelled abroad with his son. They went to

Holland and Belgium, where they viewed the site of the Battle of Waterloo. Three years later a second journey was made, taking in some of France. However, he was a very insular Englishman, and in truth the Thames at Eton and Windsor attracted him far more.

To study his style and life from his paintings, the reader cannot do better than to browse for a few hours in the Birmingham City Art Gallery and Museum. His trips to the north, to Yorkshire, Derbyshire and Lancashire resulted in inspiring studies, and in 1836 he discovered the 'Scotch' wrapping paper which is now named after him and so suited his style. The rough texture worried some viewers who were used to a watercolour being smooth, and this even had flecks in it. Once he was asked what he did if the flecks occurred in the part on which he wanted to paint sky, Cox replied rather artlessly 'I just put wings on them and they fly away as birds!' The famous *Sun, Wind and Rain* now in Birmingham has this movement and atmosphere exactly, and the wind can almost be felt in its force. Ince remained friends with him, and also with his son David all his life.

In 1841 Cox retired to Harborne, near Birmingham, then still a peaceful country place. The Coxes planned their daily routine perfectly like Trollope. He would paint, walk, entertain friends and do gardening. Sundays he would not paint and they went to church. He took up oil painting with great enthusiasm and confided to his son that it was much easier than watercolours, which is of course very true. His outings were confined to Bolton Abbey and his beloved North Wales, particularly Bettws-y-Coed. In 1845 his wife died and this was a bitter loss. He continued to paint quite profusely, probably his *Welsh Funeral* being the best known, dated 1848. He remained, the simple, kindly character he'd always been.

How lucky that Ince had been influenced by one so genuine.

4   Influences on Ince

Before Ince leaves Presteigne to set up his studio in London as an independent young painter, it is relevant to reflect on the changes that are taking place in art and particularly in watercolour painting at this time, and the influences that have determined them.

By the Middle Ages there were missals and psalters for the devout, armorial bearings for the noble, herbals and bestiaries for those seeking natural history. There were also instances of 'transparent painting', i.e. watercolour laid on over a white ground. This can be seen in illuminated medieval psalters and in the tinting in the shadows in some Old Masters. Jordaens did this to intensify his colour, so did Jan Van Eyck (d.1442) when painting with tempera (pigment mixed with egg yolk) over gesso. Rembrandt, too, was one of the first to leave his highlights on the bare paper.

England, in Tudor times, had some of the finest painters in watercolours, notably the miniaturists Nicholas Hilliard (1547–1619) and his pupil Isaac Oliver (d.1617). Later there was Samuel Cooper (1609–1672), popular in Charles II's reign; Pepys paid Cooper £38 for nine miniatures of his wife. Thereafter watercolour declined somewhat in popularity until the 18th century, when it was called 'stained drawing'. At some time John Smart (1742–1811) painted a miniature of a 'Mr Ince', but it is not dated; it is quite likely it was painted in India where Smart lived for some years and could have been of Ince's uncle who was then in India in the army of the East India Company.

There were certain artists who stamped their style indelibly on the history of art. Diego da Silva Velazquez (1599–1660), born of Portuguese parents but raised in Seville, was one of the earliest painters who dared to paint 'al fresco'; the Impressionists — coming well after Ince's time — were well aware of his interest in a naturalistic representation of scenes in sunlight and shadow. Velazquez was a successful court painter in Spain and travelled to Italy on behalf of his king, Philip IV, to buy 'only the best' of Italian paintings to add to the ever growing collection in Madrid. In his style, this discerning painter had a new kind of realistic vision. For instance, whereas Jan Van Eyck would have painted a head of hair with almost individual hairs shown, Velazquez painted the light on the pigmented tones en masse, and yet gave the impression of the colour, texture and form; we see even more than the artist presents! In his famous painting *Las Meninhas*, a Court scene with little Infantas and their retinue, he also gives a new awareness of perspective. This painting is most cleverly presented in the Prado as the viewer has a huge mirror behind him and by turning to face it finds he is 'in' the picture; he is standing exactly where the King and Queen would have stood, but they were facing the Infantas and their reflections are on the far side of the paintings itself.

Then came Claude Gellée or Claude le Lorraine (1600–1682). By the 1630s he already had a reputation as a landscape painter, which has remained undimmed throughout the centuries. He created 195 paintings called the *Liber Veritatus*, all now in the British Museum. This was not only to record his paintings, but to guard against forgery.

His landscapes are poetic, and his ideas for tonal perspective have almost become a formula. In the foreground, colours are dark and strong, the middle distance of lighter greens and the far distant areas blue, becoming paler as they recede. To emphasise this even more, he sets out 'coulisses', cleverly spaced 'side screens' as used on the stage; they could be woods, bridges, or buildings, but their effect is to take our eye back right into the heart of the picture. His paintings are the finest example of how to use tonal value and students still copy them for this reason.

This style of painting in the classic mould was the aspiration of all artists who painted landscape, nearly always as a background to legends or biblical themes. With the advent of the 18th century, subsequently well known names emerged in the field of British art, firstly Sir Joshua Reynolds (1723–1792). Well educated, he was the epitome of an English gentleman, and a friend of Dr. Johnson and Goldsmith amongst others. He left for Italy in 1849 and spent two years in Rome and here learnt the intellectual basis of classical art — and the Grand Style. He became first President of the Royal Academy and rightly so, and his portrait likenesses are meticulous.

Richard Wilson (1714–1782) the son of a Welsh clergyman and again very well educated, was soon recognised as a portrait painter of quality.

But after his two years study in Italy he devoted himself almost entirely to landscape. He was not as widely recognised as he should have been. His views of England were always in the classical style and seemed more Italian than English and they proved unpopular with collectors.

Suddenly, there was a change. Thomas Gainsborough (1727–1788) turned his gaze to the real colours of Britain. The fresh and tender greens, the changing atmosphere, the moods of the weather in an island affected nearly always by cyclonic winds. Even Gainsborough, however, could not make a living by painting landscape alone. His good fortune was that he was a sympathetic and brilliant portrait painter, and could place his figures into a landscape background.[1] Even royalty preferred his unique insight and somewhat dashing and insouciant style to that of Sir Joshua Reynolds, a style which Reynolds himself, with no bitterness, called 'the full effect of diligence under the appearance of a chance and hasty negligence'.

So comes John Constable (1777–1837) and he too, captures that unique light and strong chiaroscuro of Britain. He is influenced by the light of the early 17th century Dutch painters; but it is his own perception that holds our vision, and to which we relate.

Another artist who stamped his style on the art of the period was Joseph Mallord William Turner (1775–1837), who made the public far more aware of the beauty and fame of these islands than any other. He had a difficult boyhood, with a harsh mother from a good family, the Marshalls of Shelford Hall, Nottinghamshire, who eventually ended in the asylum. He was sent to Brentford for his health, where he learnt not only of the country but the river and was never happier than on the Thames. He knew of sails and rigging and masts, and had a sailor-like knowledge of the sea, of ripples and eddies, reflections and currents. He suffered unrequited love in his youth and the hurt undoubtedly remained with him. His brilliance at painting and swift rise to the R.A. made many jealous of him and engendered the unjust stories of meanness, when in fact he was only careful. In Walter Thornbury's book on his life, published in 1862, much is learnt from those who knew him personally: of his support of his friend Chantrey (paying the latter's rent all his life), of charity to poor houses and almshouses, his care of his father. No, he did not entertain in his home, but if a picnic was organised he was most generous and the life and soul of the party! His eyes were described sometimes as blue, sometimes as grey, but always that they were penetrating and observant.

As Professor of Perspective at the R.A. he prepared 'exquisite drawings, illustrating not only direction of light, but effects of light'. However he always had a limited ability to explain, the student having to 'read between the words'. He loved fishing, but always put anything back that was too small, and was a great bird lover; he would not let boys rob 'old black-birdy's nest'. Ruskin, the critic and writer who championed him, says 'I never knew a man freer from guile and of a kinder nature not withstanding his occasionally rough demeanour' who 'never broke a promise or failed in an undertaken task, and had a great sense of justice and fairness'.

It has been noted earlier that he had a long friendship with David Cox, calling him 'Daniel', and that he gave him a painting. It is through Cox that it is more than likely he met Ince.

At first Turner was influenced by Claude to the Classical style and produced his large paint-ings of ancient Greece, but afterwards he was moved by the sublime, those wonders of insight that his bitter enemy, Sir George Beaumont described as 'pictures of nothing and suchlike'.

In 1802, the Treaty of Amiens was signed with France. It lasted little more than a year, but it did give time for artists to go over and see for themselves in the Louvre the famous paintings that Napoleon had looted from Italy and the Low countries. Turner himself took the opportunity to see them. When he died, he bequeathed 300 paint-

Could this be a sketch of J.M.W. Turner made by Ince on a joint painting trip with Cox? The birds in the background could be a play on Turner's middle name of Mallord (mallard), which Turner himself would sometimes 'pun'[2]

ings and nearly 20,000 watercolours and drawings to the nation (National Gallery, Tate Gallery and British Museum and the Victoria & Albert Museum).

Ince was also an interested follower of the 'The Norwich School' of painters. The 'School' was founded by John Crome (1768–1821), sometimes called Old Crome, and his son John Berney Crome (1794–1842). There were some 25 other members, all of them patrons or friends. Their purpose 'was to inquire into the Rise, Progress and present state of Painting, Architecture and Sculpture, with a view to point out the Best Methods of study to attain to greater perfection in these arts'. John Sell Cotman joined the group and became Vice-President. Loving their countryside so completely, they declared that 'Nature herself was their only guide'.

John Crome's family (his father was a weaver and a publican) had been known in Norfolk for centuries. He married the daughter of a Rotterdam merchant and there were many Dutch paintings in his home. He was an excellent drawing master; teaching was his forte. These painters had a wonderful simplicity and breadth to their pictures — Crome (like Cox) also taking his classes out of doors where possible. Their style lasted over half a century and was ideally suited to the flat lands and wide skies of East Anglia, and it was obviously those skies that attracted Ince.

During Constable's time there was also a rise in popularity of the 'Sporting Artists'. After the great Francis Barlow, in the reign of Charles I, sporting art had been looked down on by the purists, but with George III (Farmer George) on the throne and increasing interest in the breeding of bloodstock and hunting, matters were to change. George Vertue, the critic, wrote of the artist John Wootton (d.1756) that he 'raised his reputation and fortune to a great height, being well esteemed for his skill in landscape painting among the Professors of Art, and in Vogue and favour with many persons of greatest Quality'. Yet Wootton, after visiting Italy, based his landscape backing for his horse paintings on Claude and the classic style, and others followed his lead causing Constable to remark humorously 'they were representing English country gentleman in their wigs, jockey caps, top boots and packs of hounds careering in Italian landscapes'! George Stubbs (1724–1806) with his unrivalled knowledge of the anatomy of the horse, together with John Fernely (1781–1860) and Benjamin Marshall (1767–1835), gradually changed this, but it was only after Henry Gordon Alken (1784–1857) that the viewer was treated to the action painting of falls, mishaps, disasters and runaways and a real English background!

What a vast number of styles, subjects and influences Ince had to consider on his arrival in London in 1826.

5   London

When Ince moved to London in 1826, he was returning to his family's roots, for his father came from a family of skilled craftsmen who had been working in the furniture trade in Covent Garden for the best part of a century. He may have initially lodged with his uncle Charles who lived in King Street, as the address from which in 1826 he submitted his first pictures for exhibition at the Society of British Artists and the Royal Academy was given as 31 King's Street, Edgware Road.

Ince's grandfather was William Ince (1737–1804), an eminent Georgian cabinet-maker. William's father was John Ince, a glass-grinder, who had a successful business of his own in Covent Garden in the years before 1745. At that time, all glass for making mirrors was still blown in the form of glass plates which were sold on to glass grinders to be finished. The grinder would trim off the unevenness at the edges, then grind away the imperfections on the surface with abrasives of varying coarseness. The final stage was to polish the glass with increasingly fine powders until a perfectly smooth finish was achieved. The glass would then be sold to a looking-glass manufacturer for silvering. The item would be completed by mounting the glass in a hand-carved wooden frame to the design and specification of the customer (or often, to that of their architect).

John Ince and his wife, Mary, had at least nine children but most seem to have died in infancy. John himself died in 1745 leaving his widow with four young children. In his Will[1] dated 3 September 1745, he sought to make provision for his family, naming as his executors other local tradesmen — John Bladwell, an upholsterer from St. Paul's, Covent Garden; Joseph Shelton, a joiner from St Martin's in the Fields; and Samuel Hoggins, a victualler also from St. Paul's, Covent Garden — in addition to his brother, William Ince. John Bladwell carried on his business in Bow Street and seems either to have been in partnership with his son, also John, or else to have been succeeded by him in the business. Certainly a John Bladwell was trading from Bow Street, Covent Garden between 1724 and 1768.[2] John Bladwell the elder married Rebecca Burrow at St. Benet Paul's Wharf on 8 June 1725. The youngest of their three children was John Bladwell junior, baptised at St Paul's, Covent Garden, on 16 January 1737, who must have taken over his father's business at the appropriate time. Their main line of work was upholstery and cabinet-making, supplying chairs, couches and beds. Their chief patron was the Duke of Bedford and furniture was provided for Woburn, but also to other great houses such as Uppark, Felbrigg and possibly Holkham Hall.

The Will of John Ince, which was proved in London on 4 October 1745, shortly after his death, shows his concern that his children should be properly apprenticed to learn a trade. The eldest son, also John, appears to have been his father's apprentice at the date of death, for the Will provides as follows:

> I will and order that my Loving Wife Mary during the Minority of my Eldest Son John shall … solely Manage and carry on my Trade and Business of a Glassgrinder and so soon as my said Son John shall attain his age of Twenty one years to admitt him as a partner in the same Business with her and Then to permit and suffer him to share the Profits equally with her in the same …

The younger surviving son, William, had been baptised on 31 March 1737 and was therefore probably 8 years old when his father died. The normal age to be apprenticed was 14 and apprenticeships lasted for seven years until the apprentice reached the age of majority at 21. Usually the master taking on an apprentice would require payment of a premium to cover the cost of board and lodging (as the apprentice would live as part of his master's household during the apprenticeship). John Ince's Will contains detailed provisions to deal with William's position and shows considerable understanding in recognising that the boy may not wish to follow his father's trade:

> it is also my Will That if my youngest Son William shall be inclined to be set Apprentice to the said Trade or Occupation of a Glassgrinder That he be and continue with his said Mother till he arrive at the age of Fourteen years and at that age to be bound Apprentice with his said Mother for the Term of seven years and so soon as he shall have served the said Term of seven years to be likewise admitted as a Partner with his said Mother and

Brother ... but if my said Son William shall not be inclined but dislike the said Business then I will and direct That the Sum of Twenty Pounds shall be given with him Apprentice to any other Trade or Business such as my said loving Wife and my Executors ... shall approve of ...

Similar provisions were made for the daughters, Elizabeth and Mary, to be apprenticed to a milliner or other suitable trade.

Events did not work out as John Ince had hoped. His son John did trade with his mother for a couple of years but he too died young, in 1748. The *General Advertiser* for 31 March 1748, a weekly newspaper sold in the London area, advertised a sale of his goods and effects at 'his late Dwelling-house' at 'the Upper End of Bow-street, Covent garden', which was to take place on 6 and 7 April 1748. The family business in glass-grinding must have come to an end upon the sale, as all of the assets employed in the trade were included in it. The advertisement detailed, in addition to finished mirrors and all the household goods, 'Likewise his Stock in Trade, viz. a Quantity of Plate-glass, from Capital Size, down to the Smallest: And all the Implements in Trade, as Large Iron Plates, Purbeck and other Stones, and Slates, for Grinding, Silvering, Polishing and Cleansing, and all other Materials in the Glass-working Business'. Presumably, Mary Ince, John's mother, had to survive after the sale on the proceeds.

William Ince, Joseph Murray Ince's grandfather, was only 11 years of age when the sale took place and he was not yet old enough to be apprenticed to a tradesman. In July 1752, however, when he was 15, William was apprenticed to John West, a cabinet-maker also in Covent Garden. West may well have been a friend of the family or of John Bladwell senior, the upholsterer who had been an executor of John Ince's Will. John Bladwell junior had been baptised less than three months before William Ince so they must have been almost the same age and, as both the Ince and Bladwell families lived and worked in Bow Street, the two were most likely close friends. It would be reasonable to draw the conclusion that William Ince's apprenticeship was arranged by his friend's father, John Bladwell senior.

John West died in May 1758, so William Ince did not serve the full seven years of his apprenticeship. However, as he had reached the age of 21, William was able to begin his own career as a cabinet-maker and did so with remarkable success.

When West died, his premises were acquired by the partnership of Samuel Norman, James Whittle and John Mayhew. William Ince must have been one of the employees of the partnership and evidently he impressed John Mayhew with his ability because, by 25 December 1758, they had entered into a partnership agreement. This partnership has been described as 'one of the most significant, probably the longest lived … of any of the major London cabinet-makers of the 18th century.'[3] Ince and Mayhew acquired the premises and stock of Charles Smith who ran a cabinet-making and upholstery business in Broad Street, Carnaby Market and on 25 January 1759 announced in the *Public Advertiser* that they were in business at that address. The partnership was intended to run for 21 years until 1780 but in fact continued until 1799, a period of over 40 years. In that year, a new partnership agreement was signed. Despite the new agreement, all was not well with the business as it struggled for cash (a recurrent feature of its history) during 1799. Perhaps the new agreement was an attempt to paper over the cracks of their differences, because less than a year later, the *London Gazette* carried a notice that on 12 April 1800 the partnership was dissolved by mutual consent. The paper also published an announcement by William Ince's son, Charles, that he would carry on business at his father's address in Broad Street, Soho.

The separation of the interests of the two partners proved to be difficult, time-consuming and contentious. Properties were mortgaged to raise £7,000 to pay off the business creditors, but realisation of the partnership assets took time. A considerable part of the partnership debts were sold at auction. Christie's held an unsuccessful sale of the stock of furniture over four days in May 1801 and a second, more successful sale in April 1804. The partnership owned substantial holdings of property including the house at Crouch End where William Ince lived and a house in Hornsey which was the residence of John Mayhew. It also owned four houses in Carnaby Market and Marlborough Row, three houses, workshops and yards in Wardour Street, two houses in Albemarle Street, three in Grafton Street and one in Sackville Street. The partnership evidently was a large and valuable business. The *Public Advertiser* carried an advertisement placed by Mayhew & Ince in July 1768 for 'upwards of 100 Men, Cabinet-makers, Chair-makers, and some very good Joyners' and for 'Some Men who can do inlaid Work in Woods &c and engrave and work in Brass'. The partnership's reputation may be judged from the fact that it charged the highest premiums for apprenticeship of all the West End furniture businesses.

William Ince had inherited a modest amount from his father, about £150, which he was due to receive on his 21st birthday, and put into the partnership only his initial share of £500. John Mayhew, on the other hand, had a private income of about £300 per annum and reckoned to have contributed about £9,000 to the business. By 1802, Mayhew claimed that £31,270 11s. 7d. was due to him whereas £6,093 6s. 8d. was due to his partner. Considerable profits had clearly been earned by both partners during the course of the business.

Mayhew's figures were, however, contested by William Ince and after his death in early 1804, by his widow, Ann, until her death in 1806. Her executors then continued the law suit in Chancery and it was still not settled at the time of Mayhew's own death in 1811. Mayhew's Will[4] may indicate how the matter was eventually settled after the death of all of the principal protagonists. In the Will itself, signed on 21 January 1811, Mayhew lamented the fact that the dispute had arisen — 'it was my earnest wish that all should be settled conformable to a Deed duly considered and established by Wm. Ince and me long before his decease' and gave his executors power 'to act as they may think most proper'. Yet only a fortnight later, in a codicil dated 9 February 1811, he advised his executors to consider settling with the Ince executors 'out of Court and without waiting the ultimate decision of Chancery' on 'just reasonable or expedient' terms.

The papers relating to the law suit have survived and show how the partnership operated.[5] Ince was involved in 'designing and drawing' and Mayhew was responsible for management of the overall business. Ince had tried and failed to keep the cash accounts from July 1760 to June 1761 and afterwards left it to Mayhew. Mayhew claimed that he dealt with the majority of the customers and spent more in entertaining them. He accepted that Ince superintended the cabinet-making side of the business but argued that they were both responsible for the business as a whole. Whatever the reality, and it must be remembered that it was in Mayhew's interest in the court case to argue that Ince was well aware of the financial aspects of the partnership, it is clear that William Ince was one of the foremost English furniture designers of his day.

Early in the life of the partnership, the partners embarked upon an ambitious folio design book. The *Gentleman's Magazine* for 13 July 1759, only six months after the creation of the partnership and just over a year after the early ending of Ince's apprenticeship, announced 'A general system of useful and ornamental furniture. By Mess. Ince and Mayhew, publishing in numbers'. The designs were to be published weekly in 40 parts from July 1759 to April 1760. The venture proved to be over-ambitious and, after delays, ground to a halt. The plates which had been completed were published in 1762 as a single volume entitled *The Universal System of Household Furniture*, dedicated to the Duke of Marlborough. The initial part work was modelled on Chippendale's *Gentleman and Cabinet-maker's Director* which had first appeared in 1754. Sadly for Ince and Mayhew, Chippendale advertised a third edition of his book as a weekly part work in October 1759. It is likely that the young partners were unable to compete effectively with Chippendale and had no alternative but to stop publishing more plates and issue their book as if it were the completed project.

The authorship of the plates in *The Universal System of Household Furniture* shows how Ince dominated the designs featured in it. Of the 101 plates (excluding metalwork designs), only 11 are signed by Mayhew; one is signed jointly; 89 are signed by Ince alone. Ince had a keen interest in furniture design and architecture. He subscribed to Chippendale's *Director*, George Richardson's *A Book of Ceilings* (1776), *Iconology* (1779) and *Treatise on the Five Orders of Architecture* (1787) and Thomas Malton's *Compleat Treatise on Perspective* (1775). He also owned a copy of Isaac Ware's *Designs of Inigo Jones* published between 1730 and 1734. In his Will, he left to his son Charles 'All my Architectural Books, Books of Furniture and Ornaments' suggesting that by the time of his death, William Ince had collected a substantial library on these subjects.

The partnership's main activity was the making and selling of furniture but its business included several other lines at various times. In trade directories and on bills, the firm advertised itself as 'cabinet-makers and upholsterers'. It also described itself as 'Manufacturers of plate glass' in 1778 and as 'dealers in plate glass' in 1799. In 1782, the firm lent the Plate Glass Company £100. This company had been established under an Act of Parliament in 1773 following a Parliamentary enquiry at which a Mr. John Mayo gave evidence. This was almost certainly Ince's partner, John Mayhew, as he was described as 'a Cabinet Maker and Worker of Plate Glass', the family connections of William Ince making the supply of fine mirror glass a natural line of business for the firm. The quality of the firm's output was recognised by a leading authority on English mirrors, Geoffrey Wills, who wrote: 'There is on the whole, little by which to differentiate an Ince and Mayhew frame from one made to the pattern of any other designer of the time, but they are able to hold their own with the best'.[6]

The partnership also let out houses which it had furnished, thereby providing an opportunity to dispose of unsold furniture which had been manufactured in the firm's workshops. As has been seen, there were several houses owned by the firm at the time of its dissolution, but it also rented property which it sublet. The firm also regularly hired out furniture for entertainments hosted by its major clients; indeed, it prided itself upon providing a wide-ranging variety of services as the firm's bills document — from supplying new furniture of the highest quality, to cleaning and repairing (in one case, for dusting the ceilings), from hanging tapestries or wallpaper to laying carpets. The firm even acted as undertakers and carried out the elaborate funeral arrangements of the third Earl of Darnley who had purchased furniture for his mansion at Cobham Hall in Kent.

Ince and Mayhew dealt with clients of the highest social class. They included the Earl of Coventry, the Duke and Duchess of Bedford, the Earl of Exeter, the Duke of Marlborough and the Duke of Devonshire. It is tempting to think that Ince's friend, John Bladwell, may have made an introduction to the Duke of Bedford who was his own principal client. The firm worked closely with architects such as Robert Adam, Lancelot 'Capability' Brown and Henry Holland, Brown's son-in-law. Mayhew culti-vated most of the relationships, but Ince was the principal contact for the second Viscount Palmerston when he was furnishing Broadlands in Hampshire, where many items supplied by the firm are still *in situ*. Other houses containing the firm's work include Chatsworth in Derbyshire, Burghley House in Lincolnshire, Kingston Lacy in Dorset and Badminton House in Gloucestershire.

It can be seen that William Ince rose from humble beginnings to become a man of high social standing. He served as a director of the Westminster Fire Office and was appointed as joint appraiser of Hartlebury Castle and the Bishop's Palace, Worcester in 1781. He had an enquiring mind and his library contained a broad range of publications including Mortimer's *History of England*, Jennings' *Geography*, the *Encyclopaedia Britannica* in 20 volumes, a *Dictionary of Arts and Sciences*, books relating to mechanics and geometry, physic and surgery (which were bequeathed to Ince's father), and a vast collection of music, both choral and instrumental (notably including Handel's *Songs and Oratorys* in 5 volumes).

Mayhew may have considered himself of higher social standing than William Ince and he had more personal wealth to invest in their part-nership, but their relationship was very close in the early years of the business. They courted and subsequently married on the same day two sisters, Isabella and Ann Stephenson, the daughters of Jane Stephenson, a widow of Hanover Square. The marriages took place by licence from the Archbishop of Canterbury at the parish church, St. George, Hanover Square on 20 February 1762. Ann Stephenson was only 19 years of age, still a minor, and the licence required her mother's consent. This she gave (although signing her name 'Jean' on the letter of consent) but could not appear in person to confirm her consent, being prevented 'by Old age and Infirmity'. Instead John Mayhew attended (as her agent) when William obtained the licence for the marriage.

After the marriage, the two couples shared the same house where the business was located at the upper end of Broad Street. The house was four storeys high and had 14 rooms, so there was no shortage of space. Isabella Mayhew gave birth to twin girls, Isabella and Sarah, who were baptised at St. James, Westminster on Boxing Day 1762. Sadly, she died in 1763 (possibly from complications) and John Mayhew moved into a nearby house in about 1764. He re-married on Christmas Eve 1765, again at St. James, Westminster, his new bride being Bridget Winsley.

William and Ann had 12 children between 1763 and 1775, of whom six, four sons and two daughters, survived to adulthood. Infant mortality was extremely high in London in the 18th century, even for those families who enjoyed a good standard of living. William and Ann, along with Mayhew, provided rooms for the firm's porters, clerks and apprentices until 1781 when they all moved in with Mayhew. The house, large as it was, must have been crowded by the time the employees moved out.

William Ince ensured that his four sons were all well provided for and able to earn a good living for themselves. The eldest, William, was born on 8 January 1764 and baptised at St. James, Westminster soon afterwards on 31 January. In 1782, at the age of 18, he was enrolled as a cadet with the military college of the East India Company.[7] At this period, the East India Company was administering India, effectively on behalf of the British Government, and had its own army. This was not formally merged into the British Army until after the Indian Mutiny of 1857. William Ince was aware of the opportunities to make a fortune open to young men in the service of the Company; two of the leading 'nabobs' — James Alexander, later 1st Earl of Caledon, and Warren Hastings, who had infamously been Governor of Bengal — were clients of Mayhew and Ince. Dedicated and able men could make their reputation in the military service of the Company, notably Arthur Wellesley, later Duke of Wellington, who made his name as a successful commander in India in the period 1798–1804.

William Ince junior took up his first commission as a lieutenant fire-worker (equivalent to the rank of ensign or second lieutenant elsewhere in the army) in the Bombay Artillery in 1783. His career suffered a setback in June 1786 when he was tried by court martial and suspended from his rank, pay and emoluments for six months. No records of courts martial for this period have survived, so we do not know the offence for which William Ince had been charged. In the event the episode proved no long term handicap as he was appointed lieutenant in 1790 and saw service in the Mysore War of 1790–1791, taking part in the sieges of Dharwar (February–March 1791), Simoga (December 1791) and Hooly Honore. Promotions were earned — to captain-lieutenant in January 1796 and to full captain in September 1797.

The situation had been quiet for a few years in India, despite the war with the French in Europe, but everything changed when Napoleon launched his attack upon Egypt in 1798. French control of Egypt would threaten British interests in India so reinforcements were despatched from England to India in late 1798 and the Bombay Artillery was sent to attack Seringapatam, near Bangalore, which fell in 1799. Captain Ince was attached to one of the two companies of artillery which were sent to Egypt from 1800 to 1802. From 1802 to 1804, he saw field service back in India in Gujerat, taking part in the capture of Baroda. At this time, Arthur Wellesley's leadership was giving the British total military control in India and creating an Indian empire.

William Ince was promoted to major in September 1804 and by 1807 had risen to the position of officer commanding the Artillery. He died at Surat, in Gujerat, on 28 September 1808, aged 44. He had never married but his Will made on 9 March 1801, which was proved before the Recorder of Bombay on 28 November 1808, sheds an interesting light on his private life.[8] It is a typical soldier's Will, direct and to the point: 'With thanks to the Almighty being in perfect Health in Body Sound in Mind I will and bequeath to my Girl Fatimah the whole of what I die possessed of after paying my just debts and I leave her my sole Executor.' The Estate Accounts of Deceased Officers for 1808–1809 coyly record that William Ince's estate was duly bequeathed 'To his female friend'.[9] As over seven years passed between the making of the Will in 1801 and his death in 1808, it is reasonable to infer that the couple had been together for a period before the Will was made, and that Fatimah Bibbee must have been William's long term partner. There is no evidence, however, that any children resulted from the relationship.

The second surviving son, Charles, was born on 9 May 1768 and baptised at St. James, Westminster on 1 June the following month. He followed his father, being trained as a cabinet-maker, and worked for his father's business. He appears to have been a partner in the Ince and Mayhew partnership when it was dissolved on 12 April 1800, when he took over his father's business. The notice placed in the *London Gazette* of 14 April 1800 read as follows:

Broad-Street, Soho, April 14 1800.
Charles Ince, Son and Successor to Mr. William Ince, of Broad-Street, Soho, begs Leave to acknowledge his Sense of Gratitude for the liberal Patronage afforded him while in the firm of Mayhew, Ince, and Sons, and now requests Permission to inform the Nobility, Gentry, and Public in general, the he purposes carrying on the Business at his Father's House, where he will deem it his first Pride to execute all Orders he may be honored with in the most exact and punctual Manner.

Charles did not achieve his father's eminence as a designer and cabinet maker and there is no trace of his business activities after 1803. He is most likely to be the Ince listed in Sheraton's 1803 *Cabinet Dictionary* at 23, Holles Street, Cavendish Square, London.

Unlike his elder brother William, Charles Ince was married with a family, having wed Anna Maria Jones at St. Anne, Soho on 23 September 1797. They soon had three children, cousins of Joseph Murray Ince — Charles Vogel born 9 October 1798, John William born 1 December 1799 and Anna Maria born 9 November 1801. The family may have moved house between 1798 and late 1799 because the eldest child was baptised at St. Pancras Old Church, whereas the younger two children were both baptised at St. Mary, Marylebone Road. Charles Ince's father stated in his Will dated 8 August 1800 that he had furnished two houses for Charles, the first in Kentish Town and the second in King Street, Portman Square, addresses that fall within the two parishes where the children were baptised.

The third surviving son was Frederick Ince born on 23 July 1769 who, like his elder siblings, was baptised at St. James, Westminster (on 23 August 1769). Frederick was set up in trade as a grocer and seems to have been in business in the City of London. His father's Will states that Frederick had had a house furnished for him 'near Saint Bartholomew Hospital in the City' and had 'the Fixtures of a Grocers Shop paid for by me'. He would appear to have had some technical training, as the Will left to Frederick

'My *Dictionary of Arts and Sciences* and Such Books as relate to Mechanics Geometry and all my Working Tools Set of Instruments in the Shagroom Case Drawing Squares &c.'

Frederick married Martha Debar on 31 August 1793 at her parish church, St. Botolph, Bishopsgate in the City of London. Martha was only 19 at the time of the marriage and her father, Benedict Debar, had to give his consent to the marriage licence. Frederick and Martha produced four sons and a daughter. The eldest, William John (presumably named after Frederick's father and grandfather) was born on 23 June 1794 and baptised at St. Mary, Marylebone on 18 July 1794. He did not survive beyond infancy, dying on 4 May 1795, aged 10 months. Henry, seemingly named after Frederick's brother, Joseph Murray Ince's father, was born on 12 January 1804. Caroline was born just a few months after Joseph Murray Ince on 15 May 1806, and was baptised together with Henry on 22 June 1806 at St. Giles, Camberwell. Edward Bret was born in 1808 and was baptised at St. Mary's, Lambeth on 16 October 1808. Percy was a late addition to the family, being born on 31 March 1818, when his mother was already 43 years old, and was only baptised when he himself was six years old, at St. Pancras Old Church on 28 November 1824. It seems that neither Frederick Ince nor his brother, Dr Ince, set much store by baptism, as his son Joseph Murray was also six when he was christened.

Frederick Ince and his family seem to have moved around London to judge from where the children were baptised. The christenings of the younger children at Camberwell and Lambeth are of note because they are the only connections between the Ince family and London south of the River Thames that have been established. Otherwise, the Ince family lived around Westminster in the 18th century and, as the 19th century passed, in the area to the north — Marylebone, St. Pancras and Hampstead.

The fourth surviving son was Henry Robert Ince, the father of Joseph Murray Ince. There were also two daughters, the elder of whom was Isabella, born on 28 February 1773 and baptised on 29 March at St. James, Westminster. She was named after Isabella Stephenson, her mother's sister, who had been Mayhew's first wife. Isabella married George Cowell on Christmas Eve 1795 at St. Mary's, Hornsey, a choice of church that indicates that William Ince had already bought the estate at Crouch End which was treated as an asset of the Ince and Mayhew partnership, and must have been living there with his wife and daughters in 1795. As William Ince was a churchwarden of St. Mary's, Hornsey in November 1793,[10] the likelihood is that they had already been there for some years. The wedding clearly had the full support of the family — the first two witnesses signing the register were William Ince (signing with his usual flourish) and his wife Ann, the third being the next person to marry into the family, the fiancée of Henry Robert Ince and future mother of Joseph Murray Ince, Ann Elizabeth Saunders.

George Cowell was a friend of the family and an executor of the Wills of both William and Ann Ince. He and Isabella lived at a house in America Square in the City of London, which was furnished and given to them by Isabella's father, William Ince, as a wedding present. They had six children, four boys and two girls. The eldest was named George, after his father, and was baptised in the nearby church of St. Botolph Without Aldgate on 22 November 1796. The next child was born on 21 December 1797 and named Isabella after her mother. She was also baptised at St. Botolph on 13 February 1798. The third child, a boy, was baptised on 15 February 1800 and was named Lambert, apparently after William Ince's banker or stockbroker. (Isabella Mayhew, the daughter of John Mayhew and Isabella Stephenson, named one of her children James Lambert Rush, so it appears that Mr. Lambert was friendly with both Ince and Mayhew, indicating that he may have been the banker to the partnership business). William Ince requested in his Will that £1,500 should be invested for his younger unmarried daughter 'in such Funds of Government Security as my good Friend Mr. Lambert …. may advise'. It can be inferred that Mr. Lambert and George Cowell were members of a close-knit group of friends of William Ince.

William Ince's youngest child was Mary Ann Ince, who was still unmarried when William Ince made his Will in 1800. No birth or baptism records have come to light for her. She did sign the marriage register as a witness when her friend, Jane Mayhew married Thomas Normansell on 14 April 1806, which suggests that despite the lawsuit between their parents, relationships between the Ince and Mayhew children remained warm.

As mentioned earlier, William Ince died in late 1803 or early 1804, so he never knew his grandson Joseph Murray Ince. William's Will[11] makes interesting reading. He showed every confidence in his wife's good sense and sound judgement as he made her an executrix of the Will, unusual at a time when married women had no property rights and could not take legal action in their own name. After making certain legacies to his children (of which more will be said later), all his personal possessions, 'my Plate

China Glass Pictures Books Prints', were to go to his wife, with those she did not want being shared among her own children 'according to her own Discretion or their Behaviour towards her'. If any of the executors died or declined to act, it was left to her 'to choose one or two other Gentlemen who she may approve on'. There was no attempt made to fetter his wife's ability to bequeath property on her death and he also wished the property held by his wife on her death to be divided 'as she pleases'. Theirs must have been a marriage which gave the wife a greater involvement in financial affairs than was the norm for the time. Perhaps this explains the confidence with which she pursued the law suit against Mayhew after William Ince's death.

William Ince believed that he had provided adequately for his children by giving them a start in life, for he left them nothing on his death. William junior had been set up in the army of the East India Company, which may have involved buying a commission, Charles had been trained as a cabinet maker and provided with furniture for two houses, Frederick had had a house and grocer's shop fitted out and Isabella had been given a house and furniture on her marriage. For the same reason, Ince's father received no inheritance on his father's death. The Will is quite explicit: 'respecting my son Henry Robert, he having had Furniture and Effects for a House in Wendover for a House in Goodge Street for a House in Grafton Street Fitzroy Square and being in a genteel profession to enable him to increase his Fortune excepting such Books as are hereafter mentioned I am hereby determined what he has had is all I mean by this Will to leave him'. Mary Ann alone had received nothing to date (as she was unmarried), so to even matters up, William left her £1,500 to be invested for her benefit.

Anne Ince evidently shared her husband's view that their sons had been adequately provided for. In her Will,[12] made in October 1806 shortly before she died, she only left them a small sum of cash, £100 to William and £50 each to the others. The residue of her estate was left equally to her daughters, Isabella, the wife of George Cowell and Mary Ann, who was still unmarried. The executors of Ann Ince's Will were the same as those chosen by her husband to administer his Will (with the obvious exception of Ann herself). They comprised George Cowell, John Cowell of the Crescent near The Minories, who may have been George's brother, and Stephen Habberton of Milk Street, Cheapside, all of the City of London. When the time came, however, Stephen Habberton renounced the position of executor and refused to act for either William or Ann Ince, the reason presumably lying in the dispute between Mayhew and the Inces. Habberton is known to have been a senior employee of the Ince and Mayhew partnership, as he receipted certain bills which have survived. He would thus have been put in a very difficult position with Mayhew, had he, as an executor, sued his former employer. He may even have still been working with Mayhew during the dissolution process.

Joseph Murray Ince did not know either of his Ince grandparents as both were dead before he was six months old. To travel to London as a young man of 20 in the hope of establishing a career as an artist must have been a daunting prospect. He had left London for Presteigne as a child, but on his return there were several Ince families with whom he could have lodged, helping him to find his feet and easing the transition from the close-knit county town to the metropolis.

Ince must have thought seriously how he was going to make his mark, and indeed his living and what the future would hold. He was not addicted to portrait painting; there are no records of him making sketches of family or friends. Nor does he want to copy, as John Scarlett Davis, his friend was doing, day after day for Mr. Young, the Keeper of the Royal Collection at Carlton House — for what, in the end turned out to be very little pay and no recognition in the catalogue when it was published. Ince loved his land-scape, he also loved buildings both for their architecture and their texture, he had a wonderful and unusual capacity for portraying surfaces, particularly of wood and stone.

He would have noted with great interest, however, that John Scarlett Davis (now in Yorkshire) was intending to publish *Twelve Views of Bolton Abbey* for which he had obtained 150 subscribers. This undoubtedly fired Ince a few years later to lithograph his famous *Seven Views of Radnorshire*.

6   The Artist Flourishes

From the list of works that Ince exhibited in London, it is easy to see that in 1826 and 1827 he must have started off with a very well stocked folio of paintings already completed, probably whilst on tour with his tutor David Cox, and during his early life in Presteigne. At the Society of British Artists in 1826 he had no less than eight paintings hung, all of which were of Wales save one entitled *Mansel Lacy in Herefordshire*. At the Royal Academy he had *Mill at Dolgelly* accepted. The following year it was an even longer list — again all scenes of Wales; in the Royal Academy there were two paintings entitled *Near Dolgelly* and *The Banks of the Lugg, Radnorshire*. This year also he showed *Village of Eardisland, Herefordshire* at the British Institution for the Promotion of Fine Arts in the United Kingdom.[1]

It was a good start for a young man of only 20. During 1826 and 1827 he must have travelled to the south coast, for among the paintings shown in 1828 are four seascapes: *Shrimpers, in Hastings* and *Selling Fish, Hastings* among the dozen shown at the Society of British Artists, *New Haven Pier* and *Seaford Point in the distance* at the Royal Academy, and *Fisherman's children on the lookout* at the British Institution. He travelled to Stockholm in 1828 because, in 1829 there are eight paintings at the Society of British Artists, this time all of them of subjects at the sea or the sea shore and two works of note, both of *The Royal Palace, Stockholm*, one of which is now in the British Museum. In the RA that year the submission was 'a study' and in the British Institution *Netley Abbey*.

It is worth looking closely at the seascapes — for an artist whose painting excursions had been more or less in the past confined to rivers and estuaries, his knowledge and observation of the sea is both accurate and instinctive. In the National Museum of Wales are two watercolours (among many others) which show this. The first is *Fishing boats in a Squall* dated 1832; a sudden squall has struck and could be dangerous to a small craft, the sea is choppy rather than having the heaving swell and undertow of a real storm. A shaft of sunlight has broken through the dark cloud and highlights the sails, indigo is used for the sea and grey brush strokes emphasise the direction of the wind. Another, called *Calm Evening off Hastings* dated 1827 could not be a greater contrast. It is a perfect benign evening of pure gold – pale gold, with only the palest of blue grey clouds on the horizon. The delicacy of these colours is never insipid, we are standing looking out to sea with a fisherman; he has had a good day, probably sold his catch, and the detail of his contented relaxation is perfect, even to the folds of his boots! His nets, draped over the prow of the boat, are drying. There is nothing else in the picture save a two-masted fishing boat on the horizon. The style of this painting is close to that of J.M.W. Turner's small subjects; it radiates peace. A further find at the National Museum of Wales was Ince's tiny sketchbook. Signed 'J.M. Ince 1829' it is leather bound, well worn and bought from S. & J. Fuller of 34 Rathbone Place and donated by C.M. Stimpson of Glyn Hall, Pontypool, who lived also in London at 59 Lewisham Park. With so little in the way of letters and documents relating to Ince, this is a gem. It shows Ince's pencil sketches to be of the very highest draughtsmanship. There is an assurance, a dexterity and mastery of line that has a magnetism of its own. There are many scenes, not all titled, but those that are include Kington church in Herefordshire (see p.21); several are by the sea. There is one in particular which seems to hold a message; it is the only 'quick' portrait found in his work — and it is a back view! A thickset man with broad shoulders is sitting hunched on a three-legged stool engrossed in sketching (see p.40). He wears a cap, full crowned and slightly nautical, and a heavy, tailored jacket with two buttons at the back on the waist. There is something about this sketch that is riveting, it dominates the page, yet there is much humour about it. For three years Ince had every opportunity of sketching David Cox on their walks together. He would not have bothered to do it now. There is a description in Walter Thornbury's *J.M.W. Turner 1862* of Turner himself, as 'short and stout with a sturdy, sailor like walk' and 'he might have been taken for a captain of a river boat steamer ...'. Dare we assume that this was indeed the great artist? His friendship with David Cox could have meant that they were all together at Hastings. It would have been a challenge to take a quick likeness of a rear view!

An undated oil painting entitled *Whitby* (Plate 23) in Hereford Museum is one of Ince's finest seascapes. There are ships of three eras, and the artist has recorded this as living history. In the far distance is a steam packet,[2] clearly showing her paddles. As early as 1824 these little ships of only 60 tons were running round the coast from port to port or on short cross channel routes. In the middle of the painting is a sailing ship, possibly a brig — she is under sail ready to catch the first tide, a merchantman carrying cargo. In the foreground a substantial rowing boat looking like a Northumberland coble, with several men on board. Ince has caught the changeover from sail to steam. The quality of light in this painting owes much to the influence of Aelpert Cuyp (1620–1691) and Salomon Van Ruysdael (1602–1670), for it has that golden glow effect which the Dutch painters used. Cuyp particularly had this way of introducing his personal light, the same kind of light that Vermeer introduced which created a magic calm out of a genre subject. Ince was an admirer of both of these artists.

In 1830 he showed a further 14 paintings at the Society of British Artists as well as having *Wood Scene, Norton, on the Estate of R. Price esq., M.P.* hung in the Academy, and *Old Buildings, Conwy* at the British Institution. The news was brought to him during the year that his mother was ill, and he hastened back to Presteigne, where she died in August.

In 1831 Ince managed to exhibit another 14 paintings at the Society of British Artists, all set in this country save *View on the Eyder, Frederichstadt on the Eyder* and *Quay at Stockholm*, which could have been painted during his earlier visit. The English scenes include some from Hampshire and Dorset such as *Calshott Castle, Isle of Wight, from Southampton Water* and *Corfe Castle, Dorset*. In 1832, Hampshire features with *Scene at Netley, Baggage Wagon – Rainy effect* hung in the Royal Academy; and 12 others which are nearly all local scenes were shown at the Society of British Artists. One of these would be most interesting historically, for it is *Scene at Cwm Elan, Radnorshire* and would be the valley before it was drowned by the reservoirs. In 1833 his exhibits at the Society of British Artists were the original paintings of the *Seven Views* in their entirety, together with *Craig Pwll Du, Radnorshire* which he was thinking of including in his second series of lithographs.

He was building up his image each year, achieving both good sales and growing recognition. The time was right, therefore, after his mother's death to tackle the *Seven Views*. There are three types of printing in art: relief, intaglio (engraving, where the lines cut into the metal are filled with ink) and flat, which uses and exploits the mutual repulsion of water and grease. The latter is lithography which, in Ince's time, used a hard stone — prob-ably limestone — well smoothed to the equal of a paper with a pleasant textured grain. Nowadays a zinc plate would be used. It is the most diffi-

Maeslwch Castle from *Seven Views*

cult of all the etching processes and was invented by Aloys Senefelder of Munich in 1798. The design was drawn on to the stone with a lithographic pencil (which has a grease content). The surface was then covered with gum Arabic and allowed to dry. The drawn image afterwards goes through various stages, including being washed, before being rolled off with ink under a heavy press. Using this technique it is possible to produce very sensitive effects and half tones and this may be why Ince chose it for his

Abbey Cwm Hir from *Seven Views*

Presteigne from *Seven Views*

Seven Views of Radnorshire. The seven subjects were: Boultibrook Bridge of Presteigne; Presteigne with the Old Town Hall; Knighton; Maeslwch Castle (the seat of Walter Wilkins esq., near Glasbury); Water-Break-Its-Neck (near New Radnor); Abbey Cwm Hir and the river Wye at Rhayader.

After his mother's death and having drawn his chosen subjects on the spot he returned to his city house and had the printing carried out by C. Hullmandel and Co., the leading printers of that time (who had actu-

Knighton from *Seven Views*

Water-Break-Its-Neck from *Seven Views*

ally done the printing of the studies of Bolton Abbey a few years before for John Scarlett Davis, Ince's friend). James Carpenter and Son of Old Bond Street were the chosen publishers, but sets could be bought by non-subscribers from other publishers including J. Wilson, the bookseller of Kington, or privately, from the artist himself.

The *Seven Views* were dedicated to the Right Hon. Lord Rodney, Lord Lieut. of Radnorshire from 1805 to 1842. His seat was Berrington Hall, a mere 12 miles from Presteigne. Lady Rodney was a daughter of the merchant banker, the Hon. Thomas Harley, the younger brother of the 4th Earl of Oxford, a most powerful family locally. The subscribers, too, were essentially well known and formed an impressive list, which may have been in no small part because Ince's father was well known socially and well liked. The list included Thomas Evans esq. of Llwynbarried, Nantmel, High Sheriff for that year, and at least seven others who would attain the Shrievalty in forthcoming years; members of 12 titled families, and no less than six members of Parliament, including Thomas Frankland Lewis esq. of Harpton Court, Richard Price esq. of Knighton (County and Boroughs of Radnor), J.C. Severn of Penybont Hall (MP for Fowey), and Edward Rogers esq. of Stanage Park (MP for Bishop's Castle). The neighbouring families of Presteigne mentioned in chapter 2 are all present, along with many others in the Church, Law, Medicine and the Army: the Reverend James Beebee, a relative of the Meyricks and Rector of Presteigne from

Plate 12 Leominster Market Hall. (Leominster Museum)

Plate 13 Jack in the Green, probably painted in 1850. (Hereford Museum)

Plate 14 Stapleton Castle. This is almost a preliminary sketch
as there are several alterations. (Private Collection)

Plate 15 Stapleton Castle. This view is from the fields to the south-east of the above
painting, and clearly shows the restored farmhouse on the castle mound.
(The Provost and Fellows, Eton College)

Plate 16 Herefordshire harvest scene, looking across Letton Lake to Hay Bluff. This painting has recently been cleaned and notice how bright are the colours. (Hereford Museum)

Plate 17 A cornfield below Ffrydd wood near Stapleton. (Private Collection)

Plate 18 Elan Valley. Note the clever composition embracing height and depth and use of the tree to frame it. (Private Collection)

Plate 19 The Mynach Falls, Devil's Bridge. Note the power given to the water by the use of broad brush strokes. (Private Collection)

Plate 20 Llanfrynach, 1849. The perfect composition! The light and shadow, the water and reflection, the figure interest and the 'Claudian' tone — so much so perfectly balanced in a tiny space. (By Permission of the National Library of Wales)

Plate 21 The Usk, Llangynidr Bridge.
(By Permission of the National Library of Wales)

Plate 22 The Wye. This was probably painted in the company of David Cox.
(Private Collection)

Plate 23 Whitby (oil), with ships of three eras (see pp. 58-59). (Hereford Museum)

Plate 24 Hastings. This was a favourite haunt of painters, not least David Cox, as the fishing boats were (and still are) hauled up onto the beach rather than kept in a harbour. (Private Collection)

Plate 25 Calm Evening off Hastings. There is exquisite detailing in the anchor and fisherman's boots, for example. (National Museums and Galleries of Wales)

Plate 26 Fishing Boats in a Squall. A shaft of sunlight breaks through the clouds onto the sails; the sea is choppy, enhancing the grey brush strokes across the sky that emphasize the winds. (National Museums and Galleries of Wales)

Plate 27 Morning. (Private Collection)

Plate 28 Evening. These two paintings are the only ones for which we have a 'recipe' of the colour mixtures in Ince's own hand.[1] (Private Collection)

Plate 29 The Shooting Party. (Private Collection)

Plate 30 A rural scene. Ince has chosen a difficult composition but achieves success with the variety in light and depth in the woodland on the right of the painting. (Private Collection)

Plate 31 Cheddar. Ince favoured the Carrier's waggon as a subject, for example see the painting on the rear cover. The waggon has broad wheels to enable it to travel through mud and the waggoner is shown walking which he had to do by law. He has his bulldog with him to act as a guard, (By Permission of the British Museum)

Plate 32 Kenilworth Castle. J.M.W. Turner remarked, whilst painting Arundel Castle, that it was 'belittled by Nature, and we see this with this picture. The beauty and form of the trees on the right, the composition of woodland in the sweep of vale all but put Kenilworth itself as just another feature. (Private Collection)

Plate 33 A Country House in Wales, but which 'sugar loaf' is in the background?
(Private Collection)

Plate 34 The house called Corton, half a mile from Presteigne. (Private Collection)

Plate 35 Cottage on the Cam. A fine example of the translucency that Ince obtains in his treatment of water. (Private Collection)

Plate 36 Tombs along the Appian Way. From Ince's visit to Italy in 1849. (Private Collection)

List of Subscribers.

Jones Mr. R.
Lewis the Rt.Hon.ble T.F. M.P. 2 Copies
Lancaster Miss
Langston Capt.
Lea Rev.d Wm
Lewis The Rev.d T.T.
Lewis Mr. R.
Loyd T.L. Esq.
Lugar R. Esq.
Murchison Roderick I. Esq.
President of the Geological Society
Meredith S.M. Esq.
Meredith Mrs.
Meredith Miss G.
Meredith Miss E.
Miles W.A. Esq.
Minors Richards Esq.
Mitchell T. Esq.
Morgan T.W. Esq.
Morgan T. Esq.
Moore T. Esq.
Moore Mr. R.
Morris T. Esq. the late
Oliver D. Esq.
Oliver Mr. S.
Price Sir Robt. Bart. M.P.
Price R. Esq. M.P.
Parsons C. Esq.
Parson Capt. G.
Peel Robt. Esq.
Pennie I.T. Esq.

Part of the Subscriber's List for *Seven Views*, this column containing the name of Roderick Murchison, President of the Geological Society

1816 to 1841; Dr. Davies who had been a doctor in Presteigne, but had moved to Kington and whose son James Edwards Davies, Barrister at Law was a personal friend of Ince and later became an Executor of his Will; Dr. Edward Jenkins, the old friend of Ince's father who had invited the family to Presteigne and owned the house in Broad Street in which they lived; and Mr. William Price, the draper of Presteigne who was also to become an Executor of Ince's Will. Members of his family are also listed: his brother, Lieut. Henry Ince and Miss Emma Philips, his little sister-in-law to be. Among others was Sir Roderick Murchison, President of the Geological Society. He and his wife had stayed several times in Presteigne during his investigations into the rock formations of the borders, researches which helped lead to his classic book *The Silurian System* published in 1838, still referred to today. One of Ince's paintings is used in the book, namely *View from Stanner Rocks*. Murchison had forged a great friendship with the aforementioned James Edward Davies who was a keen and knowledgeable fossil collector, and to whose father Murchison refers as 'my friend Dr Davies of Presteigne to whom I am indebted for valuable assistance'. Murchison's wife, Charlotte, née Hugonin, who was French (could she have been a friend of Ince's mother,

The *View from Stanner Rocks* drawn by Ince, from a copy of *The Silurian System*
in the possession of Mr. Alan Lloyd

Anne Elizabeth?), has been described as 'thoughtful, cultivated and affec-
tionate' and was herself no mean landscape artist for two of her paintings
also illustrate her husband's book: *View of Breidden Hill from Powis Castle* and
Carneddau Hills from near Builth.[3]

Another subscriber was John Hinxman esq. who lived in Finchingfield
in Essex and became the generous patron of John Scarlett Davis, in fact
it would not be difficult to assume that if it had not been for Hinxman,
Davis might have starved. For the whole of his life, according to the historian G. Watkin Williams, 'his most generous and consistent patron was
John Hinxman, a wealthy merchant and naval agent, from whom the artist
had received £200 a year and all his travel and living costs', no mean sum.
Hinxman may have had his attention drawn to the *Seven Views* by Scarlett
Davis and, being a keen collector would not have missed out.

Not only should the *Seven Views* have made a good profit for Ince, just as
importantly it would have made his name known. Some of the subscribers
had more than one copy, Lewis of Harpton had two, Lord Rodney three,
Sir Harford Brydges two, Wilkins of Maeslwch Castle five, and the print
and booksellers in London such as Bohns, Moltens and Graves, and Fullers
had several.

7 Presteigne and Family Affairs

Fresh with his success of the *Seven Views* he married a lady he must have known for several years, Sarah Phillips of Presteigne. Sarah, or Sally, was a daughter of Thomas Phillips, a native of Ruabon, whose wife was Elizabeth, daughter of James Cross of Hanwood, Shropshire. The Phillips were a well known family in Shrewsbury. In 1828 they are recorded as glove manufacturers of Bell Lane, they were also drapers in the High Street in premises next to the Unitarian Chapel. John Frankwell Phillips had been a builder and it was his son, Thomas, who was living at Preston Boats when his daughter Sarah was born on 3 May 1800. There would have been plenty of building work to be done at that time with the advent of canals. Thomas was styled as a painter, of the interior decorator variety, in the births records. Sarah was baptized in Upton Magna Church, as were her subsequent sister Ann and her brother Edward. Thomas must have arrived in Presteigne around 1820 for William, his youngest son, was born there in 1822 and Emma, his youngest daughter, in 1824. In all there were eight children, but three died young. William left Presteigne at 12 years of age to join his older cousins and brothers at the shop in Shrewsbury, now undertaking high class tailoring, and specialising in 'habit making' and 'breeches making'. The firm of J.E. & W. Phillips was so successful that it was appointed military outfitters to the army, Shrewsbury being the headquarters of the 53rd Regiment of Foot (the Shropshires) and the Shropshire Yeomanry. Ince may have helped financially, but the Phillips family had undoubtedly prospered. The house in the High Street is now part of a branch of Debenhams, but is still a handsome building of two storeys and being largely half timbered it is listed.

The wedding took place in London at St. Mary's church, Marylebone on 12 June 1834. Ince had obtained the marriage licence from the Vicar General's office in London two days earlier. He stated that he was a resident of the parish of St Mary's, and gave Sarah Phillips as a resident of Presteigne. That the wedding took place in London suggests that Ince had a large circle of friends there.

From the evidence from Ince's later paintings it looks as though he and Sarah then journeyed to Devon for a long holiday and on the way back they stayed in Clifton, Bristol. After a while in Presteigne they travelled up to London and thence to Oxford, where Ince again busied himself painting. The sketches for these are now in the National Museum of Wales, over 40 drawings in all; they are valuable records of Oxford at that time and Ince may have had ready buyers for them amongst the undergraduates. They also spent a few weeks in Cambridge as his *Caius College Chapel interior* and *Gate of Honour Caius College* are also dated 1834.

Ince also arranged to exhibit the Devon paintings and two of Bristol that year, perhaps he and Sarah viewed them together. At the Society of British Artists were *Street Scene Clovelly, North Devon, Street Scene with the Guild Hall and Christ Church, Bristol, Clovelly from the Pier, North Devon, Wildasmouth Cliff, near Ilfracombe – Twilight, Clifton, Rocks near Ilfracombe*. Two that year were hung in the Royal Academy, *Lundy Island from Sir James Hamlyn-Williams' Grounds, near Clovelly* and *Moonlight, Clovelly – Ferry Boats in Bideford Bay*. In the British Institution was *Lane seen near Ilfracombe*. By the late autumn of

The tomb of Ince's wife. Sarah, and their baby daughter in Presteigne churchyard, with Roselands, the house in which Dr. Ince lived, in the background

1834, Sarah was pregnant and they journeyed back to Presteigne, perhaps to be near her mother.

In May 1835 Sarah gave birth, probably prematurely, to a son, Henry (after his grandfather) Joseph (after his father). It was a terrible time. The baby survived until 27 July, nine weeks later, and Sarah, who had herself been dangerously ill since the birth, died only two weeks after her little son's death on 9 August 1835. Sarah was six years older than Ince, but still only 32, a young woman. It was a double tragedy; long drawn out, with hopes rising, finally only to come to nothing, but sadly an all too common occurrence in those days. The baby was buried with his mother, and the stone, a simple square shape is on the east of the old churchyard, within sight of Ince's house in Broad Street. As soon as he could Ince moved back to London, away from the well meant sympathy of Presteigne. At around this time he received two letters from John Scarlett Davis.

It is interesting to quote from these letters. Davis had been commissioned to record the library of Benjamin Windus, a retired coach maker and a great collector of J.M.W. Turner's paintings. The letters are printed in Walter Thornbury's book on Turner but sadly as this book, either the first or second volume, had no references, it is impossible to find out where they are. The earlier of the two notes: 'I am working on a very difficult subject, the interior of a library of a Mr Windus, who has filled it with about 50 Turners, when you come to town we will go down to him I can assure you a treat. There are parts of some of them wonderful, and by God all other drawings look heavy and vulgar even Callcot and Stanfield (even the immortal Vicars, Harding and Pyne)'. In the second he writes 'I know it will give you great pleasure that Turner has seen it [his drawing] and spoken in the highest terms of it and that it now hangs in company with 50 of his best works'. He goes on 'I have no artistical chat for you, further than that Turner has painted a large picture of the Burning of the Two Houses of Parliament; but I have heard it spoken of as a failure — a devil of a lot of chrome [yellow]. He finished it on the walls the last two days before the Gallery opened to the public. I am told it was good fun to see the great man whacking away with about 50 stupid apes standing around him, and I understand he was cursedly annoyed the fools kept peeping into his colour box and examining all his brushes and colours'. These letters could have been written to try and give a little sympathy and cheer to his friend. John Scarlett Davis always wrote with a schoolboyish idiom and had a rare humour in his description.

Drawings of trees by Ince in 1846.[1]
All the studies on the next four pages
are on tinted paper with highlights in
white gouache

Ince now had no enthusiasm for a second *Seven Views* of parts of Wales although he had earlier drafted out his ideas, and even made some sketches. They would have been: Stannage Castle. The Pass at Cwm Elan, Aber Edwr, Old Castle Bridge (on the Ithon two miles north-east of Llandrindod Wells and now known as Alpine Bridge), The Waterfall near Maeslwch (Craig-pwll-du which Sir Roderick Murchison described as 'a narrow mountain gorge in which the Bach Howey falls over a vertical cliff'; an awesome and inspiring spot, quite difficult to reach, it lies about four miles north-west of Maeslwch) and 'other scenes equally picturesque'. Devil's Bridge would have certainly been one of them, as he had already painted this scene (see plate 19). Possibly Ince would also have chosen the Gorge at Kinsham, showing the Court up above; and perhaps Stanner Rocks too.

His London exhibits of 1835 in the Society of British Artists were *View from Winchcliffe, looking towards Bristol Channel* and *Llanelltyd Vale and Village with Heugwrt Hall, and the Junction of Dolgelly and Llanelltyd rivers forming the Barmouth river, taken from above the woods to the left of the road from Dolgelly to Arthog, North Wales*, a quite unusually detailed description. Nothing was exhibited at the Royal Academy and only *Glen on the Edw, Radnorshire* and *Scene near Maentvorog* at the British Institution.

The following years his exhibits for 1836 at the Society of British Artists again numbered two: one of *Twickenham Looking up the River* (now at Eton College) and the important painting of *Caius Gate of Honour Gonville and Caius College, Cambridge*, already mentioned. This was sold by Christies in 1986. It is signed and dated 1834 and had been in the same family since it was painted. It is now at the Fitzwilliam Museum. Hung at the Royal Academy was *Old Houses, Leominster.* Now in a private collection, it shows some beautiful ancient, half-timbered houses leading off Corn Square, and is an important record as they have now been pulled down. During the year he returned to Oxford to complete his series of Oxford College scenes.

The malign fates, however had not finished with Ince yet and in 1836 he received the news that his father had been presented with a son by their housekeeper, Mary Ann Young. His father would have written to tell him; it was certainly not an unknown situation. Mrs. Young had been housekeeper to the family for some years and was aged 43, the doctor was a hale and hearty 64 years of age (he lived until he was 78), and it was six years since Ince's mother had died. He had acknowledged pater-

nity and obviously agreed to his responsibilities financially. The baby was christened by the rector, the Rev. James Beebee — a very old family friend, and Presteigne lifted no eyebrows.

At that time, Ince was spending part of the year in London, and part of the year sketching in Wales. When he was told of Mary's pregnancy, he must have had mixed emotions. His own infant son, Henry Joseph, had been buried only months earlier in July 1835, followed to the grave in August by his wife. It is a tribute to his generosity of spirit that he was to treat his illegitimate brother with the same consideration that he treated his full brother, Henry.

The baby's parentage was acknowledged from the outset, Dr. Ince making no attempt to disguise the fact that he was the father. The choice of names for the baby — Edward Ince — made that clear. The baptism record also makes a frank description of the situation: 'Edward Ince illeg. son of Mary Young'. Mary Young continued as housekeeper for Dr. Ince and the baby was brought up by both its parents. The 1841 census reveals that the household in St. Davids Street consisted of Dr.

Ince, Joseph Murray Ince, Mary Young 'house servant' and the 4-year-old Edward Young.

In 1837 most of Ince's eight contributions to the Society of British Artists were of subjects local to Wales, but the two that were hung in the Royal Academy were again of Devon: *At Lynmouth, North Devon looking towards the Welsh Coast* and *Street Scene, Ilfracombe looking to Hillsborough Cliffs*. Ince was being hung regularly at the Academy now. Whether he would have been elected an Academician is not known, for he never applied, but on the basis of his successes it certainly would have been more than a possibility.[2]

By the end of 1837 Ince had decided to return to Presteigne for a while and an ideal opportunity presented itself. For some time there had been many ill-tempered factions in the town. In 1836 Sir Harford Jones-Brydges of Boultibrook, from all accounts an irascible gentleman, whose great wealth had been accrued in The East India Company, had put forward his cousin, Whitcomb, to be Medical Officer of the Poor Law Union. Cecil Parsons, a well known local solicitor, had unsuccessfully backed Dr. Ince and the local chemist, Mr. Vincent Cooksey, who also acted

as the vet (a not unusual combination). However, within a year Whitcomb had been dismissed, and Dr. Ince appointed. A letter written in the *Lancet* during this period could have been described as slanderous, for it referred to Dr. Ince as an 'old army surgeon whose infirmities incapacitated him in the performance of his duties' — this does not seem to fit the good doctor, a hale and hearty 64 year old who had just fathered a child. Furthermore it was Dr. Ince who founded the Committee, set up in 1834, to arrange for the first lighting of the town's street lamps by oil. The description of Vincent Cooksey was even worse, depicting him as no more than a 'quack'. The stage was well set and the antagonism still there, when Cecil Parsons, fighting the Enclosures Act of 1836 and the local large landowners, had gone to the Court of Common Pleas at his own expense — and won! In doing so he saved the livelihood of over two hundred of the poorest cottagers who had been threatened with eviction from their tiny crofts. Some of the evictions already carried out in the vicinity had been cruel in the extreme. In Llanyre a family called Weale were thrown out, the wife having only just delivered her third baby and too weak to walk — this in the middle of February.

To celebrate this legal victory a party was planned at the Radnorshire Arms, Presteigne on 20 December 1837, described at length three weeks later in the *Hereford Journal* (taking up two and a quarter columns of broadsheet). There were over 70 people present, and many were the speeches; Cecil Parsons said 'if you turn a poor man out of his little holding of land you make him an outcast of society, and a ready agent for the commission of any crime. (here, here!) It was a case between the weak against the strong (applause!).' Arthur Wall of Knill was the chairman, and he too made a stirring speech. Toasts were drunk (with three times three and one cheer more!) The Reverend James Beebee, now aged 84, replied for the church, but left early, as he was by now rather frail. All the 'neighbours' mentioned in the earlier chapter of this book were there. 'The Ladies of Radnorshire' were toasted many times! There was a song, sung by Captain Stephens, and later another one sung by Mr. Price (the draper). A Mr. Jenkins who had ridden some 20 miles to get there and was of the Dissenters of Radnorshire said 'I am a Welshman — you can tell by my speech — let us give our mite to this cause! (loud cheers)' and predicted that 'The name of Parsons will be lisped by the poor children of the Radnorshire hills'.

Cecil Parsons himself proposed the toast to Dr. Ince. The latter most probably had been doing what he could in a medical way for those

The Radnorshire Arms in Presteigne

suffering families who had been displaced. This then was a very good moment for Ince to have returned to his Presteigne home for a while, accompanying his father to the party. The gathering, after presenting a handsome goblet and salver to Cecil Parsons, continued their rejoicing unabated until 9.30pm. At Presteigne church the bells 'rang merrily.' There were bonfires in the street with some of the effigies strangely resembling the landowners! An injunction of riotous behaviour was brought against Presteigne by the authorities but nothing came of it.

There were further family troubles to come, this time for Ince's brother, Henry. Ensign Henry Ince had been commissioned as a lieutenant in the Berkshire Militia on 2 July 1821. His military career was scarcely glorious, although he remained on the nominal strength of the regiment until 1852. A national programme to reform the militia was put into effect that year as a result of the coup d'état of Louis Napoleon in France the previous December which had created alarm in London. The return of the officers of the Berkshire regiment of militia showed Henry Ince to be one of no less than six lieutenants. In fact, none of the lieutenants were rated 'effective' for military service and when the militia was called out for training, Henry Ince resigned his commission in October 1852.

Henry had returned to Presteigne after the end of the Napoleonic Wars. He married a Presteigne girl, Charlotte Vaughan Roe, in Swansea on 16 July 1826. The connection between the couple and Swansea is unclear and their reasons for marrying there are unknown. The marriage record states that both were then resident in the parish of St. Mary Swansea but its significance is diminished by the fact that 'residency' was achieved after only 14 days.

Henry and Charlotte had nine children of whom six survived past infancy. We can deduce where the children were born by tracing their census entries in later years. The eldest, yet again a Henry Robert Ince, although he seems to have been known as Robert, was born in Tring, Hertfordshire in 1827. The next child, christened in both Knighton and Presteigne in

1829, was Edward Joseph, born in Knighton in late 1828 or early 1829. The Knighton baptism entry shows that they were living in 'Garth Cottage near Knighton' in January 1829. By 30 September 1829 the family had established themselves in Broadheath near Presteigne. The baptism register of St. Andrew's, Presteigne records that Henry Robert Ince and Edward Joseph Ince were both christened on that day. It would be wrong to jump to the conclusion, as does Oliver,[3] that this means the children were twins. Baptismal records of the period generally state whether multiple christenings are of twins or triplets and in the case of the Ince children, we can establish their ages from the 1841 census.

The family at Broadheath grew with the births of Ann Susan Charlotte (baptised on 29 March 1830) and George Sanders (baptised on 20 April 1831). The baptism records at Presteigne describe Henry Ince as 'Gent.', implying that he did not work for his living. It is suggested by Oliver that he farmed one of the three Broadheath farms owned by J. Edwards, Esq which is certainly the most likely explanation. In about 1831, he appears to have given up farming at Broadheath, because by 1832 he had moved into the house in St. Davids Street rented by his father. His mother, Anne Elizabeth Ince (née Saunders), had died in August 1830 and with brother Joseph away in London, there was sufficient room for Henry, Charlotte and their young family.

In memory of Henry's mother, the first girl born at St. Davids Street was christened Anne Elizabeth Saunders Ince (on 30 April 1832). She died aged only 20 months, being buried on 5 February 1833. Two further boys were baptised on 30 April 1836, Thomas and Horatio James. The register makes it clear that these children were not twins as it specifies Thomas's date of birth as 23 April 1834. Horatio was presumably born in 1836. Harriet Ann Elizabeth was the last child to be born and baptised in Presteigne, being christened on 25 March 1838.

Henry's lifestyle as a gentleman farmer, without a private income (other than from his militia commission), was not sustainable in the long term and it appears that his financial situation had become perilous by the winter of 1838/39. He appears to have solved the crisis by moving away from Presteigne for a time, leaving his father and brother to sort out the mess. The *Hereford Journal* carried a notice dated 14 January 1839 announcing 'Modern and Elegant Household Furniture, Farming Stock, Crops, Implements of Husbandry, &c. &c' to be sold at auction over two days. There seems to have been a complete sale of all 'Captain' Ince's personal effects, as he is referred to in the advertisement, including 'valuable and superb furniture' (some of it possibly made by the partnership of Ince & Mayhew). It even included a meat safe and a child's crib, which implies that Henry and Charlotte had taken with them only what they could carry. The notice suggests Henry had continued farming, even when living in St. Davids Street, as the farming stock, 'which has been selected by Captain Ince, with much choice' included 80 sheep, 2 horses, 11 head of cattle, 12 pigs, 10 tons of hay, wheat, oats, peas and potatoes. From this, we can deduce that Henry Ince was farming on a reasonably large scale.

Yet he was evidently unable to make ends meet. The notice in the *Hereford Journal* concludes 'The Creditors of Capt. Ince are requested to leave their accounts under Cover, at my Office before the 30th instant. W. Stephens, Solicitor, Broad Street, Presteign.' No evidence has come to light that Henry Ince was declared bankrupt and so he appears to have avoided that stigma. He may have staved this off by obtaining a loan from his father, but if so, the funds appear to have been provided by his brother, Joseph. Under the terms of his Will, made in June 1838, Dr. Ince left to Joseph all his 'household furniture, plate, linen and china in consideration of him having lent me the sum of two hundred pounds'. He named Joseph his sole executor with the duty to divide the estate equally with his two brothers, Henry Robert and Edward Ince Young. The clear implication is that Dr. Ince regarded his second son, Joseph, as more responsible financially than his elder son, Henry (Edward was only 2 years old in 1838). Whilst Dr. Ince had his army pension, his earnings as surgeon to the Radnor County Gaols and medical officer to the Presteigne Poor Law Union, together with any monies earned from private practice, the list sounds more impressive than it was. The gaols only paid 5 guineas per quarter plus costs, and it was alleged in the previously mentioned letter in the *Lancet* that Dr. Ince's infirmities incapacitated him from performing his duties as medical officer,[4] requiring him to employ a deputy and suggesting that any private medical practice would not be substantial.

After leaving Presteigne, Henry Ince took his family to Swansea. His wife Charlotte was pregnant which suggests that the move was made in a hurry and was forced on him by his financial circumstances. Presumably Charlotte's family had moved to Swansea and were able to give the Ince family a place of refuge. Charlotte gave birth to the youngest child, William Henry, on 24 May 1839 who was christened at St. Mary's, Swansea on 30 June 1839.

Henry did not keep his family away from Presteigne for long as they appear to have returned as soon as they decently could. By the time of the 1841 census, the family was living in a house at Clatterbrook, the Slough. The entry shows Henry Ince's occupation simply as 'Army'. Strangely there is no sign of his wife, Charlotte, although there is a lady in the house, Anne Vaughan, aged about 70, who may have been Charlotte's aunt, her mother's sister. The eight living children are mentioned. The parish registers record that Henry and Charlotte were living at Dolley Green in May 1843 when their daughter Harriet was buried, dying at the age of 4 years. Where the family moved next is a mystery; despite extensive searches no sign of the family has come to light in the 1851 census of England and Wales. Their son Thomas was the only member who remained in Presteigne at that time. Aged 17, he was apprenticed to a master bootmaker, James Meredith, and lived with the Meredith family in the High Street. The whereabouts of the rest of the Ince family cannot be traced. Did Henry Ince take his family abroad for a time in a failed attempt to build a new life in one of the British colonies?

By the time of the 1861 census, Henry and Charlotte can be found in London, living in rooms at 4 Newberry Place, St Pancras[5] and close to 9 George Street, Marylebone where Joseph Murray Ince had died in 1859. The informant noted on the death certificate was 'C. Ince', most probably Charlotte, also of 9 George Street. It seems that Henry and Charlotte may have shared the artist's rooms for a while. Perhaps Charlotte nursed him as his condition deteriorated.

Joseph Murray Ince made generous provision for Henry and Charlotte and their children in his Will. He left £1,000 of 3% Reduced Annuities on trust, the interest arising being paid to Henry and Charlotte for their joint lives. This would have ensured that they had a roof over their heads. It is instructive that the money was put in trust and not given directly to Henry; presumably Joseph's past experience of his elder brother's profligacy led him to conclude that it would be better that he received £30 each and every year, rather than spending his way through £1,000 in short order.

Whilst helping to resolve his brother's financial problems, it seems that in 1838–1839 Ince, from his paintings exhibited and those in private ownership, travelled extensively throughout Wales. He was lucky to leave Presteigne early in the year, for in June 1838 a 'most disastrous' flood struck the town. The Clatterbrook overflowed with such force the water surged down from Green End, carrying huge beams from Robert Lewis' timber yard and cascading down Broad Street several feet deep, towards the River Lugg (it already having burst its banks). The Toll Gate on the Coombe road was swept away and the Toll Keeper rescued with 'much difficulty' from his little house. It was reported in the *Hereford Journal* of 18 June that this flash flood had 'such terrific force it lasted several hours', and that afterwards holes 4 feet deep were left in the roadway.

In 1839 Ince had written a long letter to John Scarlett Davis, for the latter, writing to his brother Francis in a letter from Venice dated 9 March 1839, says 'letters here are charged by weight. The one from you and my friend Ince cost me as much as seven of Mr Hinxman's because of the thickness of the paper!'

In 1837 Ince had exhibited three paintings at the British Institution — *Entrance in Oxford by High Street, Cattle in a Marsh,* and *Lane Scene in Devon* — but after his time in Wales it is likely that he travelled to Holland and Germany, for he did not exhibit at all between 1838 and 1840. In 1841 Ince resided at 9 George Street, Portman Square having moved from nearby 48 George Street. He worked away as busily as ever, although exhibited less, and it would seem that he had moved to a place with a bigger studio where he would complete many of his Oxford studies and larger paintings. The following year he shows no less than seven paintings at the Society of British Artists, three of them being *Windmill near Rotterdam, Oberwessel and Schomberg Castle on the Rhine* and *Off the Reculvers,* each the result of recent journeys. Another of the paintings, the important *Scene near Dolgelly on the Barmouth Road, north Wales,* (now in Hereford Museum) was hung in the Academy. *Interior of Trinity College Hall, Cambridge* (now in the Fitzwilliam Museum) was in the British Institution exhibition and in 1843 was acquired by Queen Victoria.

A letter from Scarlett Davis dated 1 January 1841 from Amsterdam, and written to his mother and brother Francis, notes 'I saw my friend Ince when in London'. Scarlett Davis and his wife had just set off on a painting tour on the Continent. To give some idea of the hardship of travel in those days, Scarlett Davis goes on in his letter 'we left last Wednesday in the packet for Rotterdam, on account of ice we were obliged to go higher up the coast to Scheuching, but as the sea was running too high to get into the bay we were taken out (a fishing vessel having come to our assistance) and afterwards carried through a heavy surf on the backs of men to the beach in safety but with a good ducking.' One can only imagine those icy waters of the North Sea. Davis and his wife eventually reached Rome where his commission from Hinxman was to paint a very large oil, measuring seven by nearly ten feet, of the interior of St Peter's. They travelled back with this painting by way of Terny, Spoleto, Perugia, Florence, Lucca, Genoa, Nice, Avignon, Lyon and Paris, arriving in Boulogne on the 26 May 1842 'much fatigued'. In fact, Scarlett Davis was now very unwell; by the summer they were housed at Sudbury Court, Harrow, which Hinxman had taken for them, and the family were all together.

Davis' great painting was exhibited in 1844 at the British Institution and very well received. Ince would have rejoiced with him. He, himself that year had shown *Ragland Castle across the Moat* and *On the Thames below Woolwich, moon rising* at the Society of British Artists, and the previous year had *Windmills in Rotterdam* hung at the Royal Academy and *Scene of Dolgelly* at the British Institution.

Ince and Scarlett Davis may have talked of having some good fishing together in the near future for the latter wrote to his mother on 24 July 1843 from Sudbury asking her to 'tell Francis to get his tackle ready for I intend to kill more fish in the obscure Lugg than I ever did in the Tiber or Po'.

In 1842-43 Ince had been back painting in Cambridge when the town was visited by Queen Victoria. 'The Visit of her most Gracious Majesty Queen Victoria, to the University, County and Town of Cambridge, October

A View from Trinity Bridge, Cambridge

1843' rang the headlines of the *Cambridge Chronicle*. The report of this visit of Queen Victoria and Prince Albert covers two whole broadsheet pages in small print. Written in the flowery and beautiful English of the time it makes for wonderfully entertaining reading. The journey to Cambridge was by carriage, the Royal Carriage followed by the Aides and Ladies in Waiting, and another with 'her majesty's suits'. Every six miles there was a

The Fountain, Trinity College

change of horses, and at Tottenham, Waltham Cross, Ware and Buntingford the military escort was changed too. By the time the cavalcade arrived in Cambridge it numbered over 2,000 as country gentlemen joined in.

Queen Street, Cambridge by Ince — one side of the street

The Queen arrived at Trinity College where she was staying at Trinity Lodge 'at a quarter before two o'clock' to the sound of the bells of St. Mary's. Speeches of welcome followed, and in the early evening the Royal

Queen Street, Cambridge by Ince — the other side of the street

From a series of drawings and engravings made by Ince of Cambridge in 1838:
Top left: Hobson's Conduit; Top right: The Round Church
Bottom left: Trinity Hall Street; Bottom right: In Trinity Street

couple were at King's College Chapel for a special service. Victoria then expressed a wish to see Trinity Chapel, and this caused 'a little bustle and momentary confusion', as she had not been expected there — and even the gates were not open. The red carpets had been taken up in order to leave a space clear for the Royal carriage to drive to the Lodge, and these had now to be relaid. However, a large gap of uncarpeted space was left, but the undergraduates, forming a double line each side of the route 'at a word' took off their gowns and laid them on the ground for her Majesty to walk across. They thus became the 19th-century equivalents of Sir Walter Raleigh! The Queen was amused and gratified and noted the details in her personal diary.

The Royal visit was an enormous success — even the weather held — and the next day was closely packed with official visits. Before leaving, five paintings of the colleges were 'acquired' for the Royal Collection. These were *Trinity College Chapel, Interior looking East* (dated 1842); *Trinity College Library, North Side*

Milton's Mulberry Tree, Cambridge

The Pepys Library, Magdalen College

(dated 1842); *St. John's College* (dated 1843); *Trinity, Interior of Hall* (dated 1835) and *The Senate House Passage* — all by Ince. In 1937, King George VI, then studying history and economics at Trinity College, presented them back to the Fitzwilliam Museum, where they are now.[6]

Organised cricket had meantime reached the borders, and there is an account in the *Hereford Journal* of the first cricket match between Presteigne and Kington, held on Thursday 18 July 1844. Kington was a rival both in commerce and sport, as well as being 'over the Border'. The match was played on the Broadheath, an ideal pitch as well as having the Cat and Fiddle and the new hostelry, The Cricketers, to help along with the liquid refreshment. According to the *Journal* 'the meeting was characterised by conviviality and good feeling' and that 'owing to the novelty of cricket in this locality, there was a large attendance on the ground.' In the batting list there is a Mr. Ince who made four runs; no initials are given so it could have been the old doctor, but more likely our artist. Kington won by four wickets and ten runs, so doubtless Presteigne drowned their sorrows!

Ince's travels later seemed to take him towards Brecon for he painted *Hay and the Brecon Beacons* (now in Hereford Museum), along with *The Quarry* (now in the National Museum of Wales). John Scarlett Davis was now very ill from tuberculosis and was staying with his brother Edmund, curate at Llangattock. Most certainly Ince would have visited him either there or later at Llanthony Abbey where Scarlett Davis went for a time seeking rest and meditation. In the autumn Scarlett Davis went back to London but never regained strength and died on 29 September 1845 aged only 41.

Ince had lost an old friend; although their paths took different routes, they had always corresponded, and met whenever possible. That last fishing trip they had both looked forward to, never took place. Ince seemed to have kept an eye on Scarlett Davis' family and made sure they did not want. Indeed, in his Will, he made provision for Mrs. Davis, leaving her over £1,000.

In 1845–1846 Ince completed *Atcham Church* (now in Hereford Museum), Atcham being where Sarah, his late wife, had been born. He also painted *Valley of the Llugwy* and *Hay-on-Wye and the Brecon Beacons* (both in Hereford Museum), each of them in oils. Other paintings of the period are held by the Fitzwilliam Museum — the oil *Fountain Court,* and watercolours of *Queens College Cambridge, The Round Church, Cambridge* and *Interior of Hall, Trinity College* — whilst the oil *Ragland Castle* is held by Hereford Museum. None of these were exhibited.

During 1847–1848 in London he exhibited *Cottages at Presteigne*, hung in the Academy, *Warwick Castle from the Town Bridge* at the Society of British Artists and *Ludlow Castle from the opposite bank of the Teme, looking up Corve Dale* at the British Institution. In 1849 he was preparing to show *Cader Idris from the Barmouth Road* and *Part of the Fitzwilliam Museum, Cambridge* when the news of his father's death was brought to him. Admittedly Dr. Ince was 78 years old, but his life ended quite suddenly, he had had angina and he died of a heart attack. He had been visiting Mrs. Young at West Walls, just off St. Davids Street. It appears that he was renting the house for Mary and her son, because the death certificate describes her as an 'inmate' of West Walls, clarifying the description by explaining 'occupier deceased', presumably Dr. Ince. The original old cottages led right down to the river Lugg but have now been pulled down. Dr. Ince's own residence was still in St Davids Street as is confirmed by the burial register of St. Andrew's church, Presteigne and by the death notice placed in the *Hereford Journal* on 28 March 1849. This discreetly, if somewhat inaccurately, states that the death took place 'at his residence, in St. David-street, Presteign'.

As has been mentioned, on his death Dr. Ince had entrusted Joseph Murray Ince, as executor, to divide the estate equally between the three sons: Henry Ince, Joseph Murray Ince and Edward Ince Young. This was specified without regard to their legitimacy or otherwise and again demonstrates how Dr. Ince accepted fully the obligations of paternity.

Ince had to go to Presteigne and decide exactly what to do. The family had never owned a house; in the 1845 tithe appointment for Presteigne parish they do not appear as owners or even occupiers of land. (Incidentally, not being a property owner would have disqualified Dr. Ince from becoming a magistrate or holding office as High Sheriff.)

In the event Ince decided very quickly what course he was going to take. He had come to a time in his life when everything had changed; with the death of his father the family connections with Presteigne had been severed with the exception of his half-brother. He still had many friends of his own age there of course, but by now most of them were married with their own young families. His brother Henry had moved away and old Dr. Edward Jenkins had died in 1843. Just one month after his father's death, Ince arranged a sale of his furniture to be held in Presteigne under the auctioneer Walter Bluck. This is interesting, for nowhere else in the *Hereford Journals* of the time is there any other reference to this gentleman as an auctioneer; nearly all the farm and property sales were carried out by John

Wilson or Thomas Price. It is a fair assumption therefore that Walter Bluck had been brought down especially from London, and was, quite possibly, a friend of Ince. This sale on 17 April 1849 shows that Dr. Ince's house contents were both elegant and interesting (see newspaper list overleaf).

It does not say in the *Hereford Journal* whether these were removed to the Radnorshire Arms Hotel, therefore they could well have been sold on site at Roselands, where Dr. Ince lived in Broad Street. On Wednesday 18 April 1849, again under the hammer of Walter Bluck, there was the following notice 'In the large room of the Radnorshire Arms Hotel, removed for convenience of sale from the residence of the late H.R. Ince esq., a valuable collection of OIL PAINTINGS, water colour drawings, prints etc and etc the property of J.M. Ince esq., who is removing to a distance'.

The prints look to be the sort that would be hanging in any well to do Georgian home. The watercolours, crayon, and body colours

PRESTEIGN, RADNORSHIRE.

Excellent HOUSEHOLD FURNITURE, superior Feather Beds and Bed Linen, handsome Chimney Glasses, curious old China, rich cut Glass, valuable LIBRARY;

TO BE SOLD BY AUCTION,

By WALTER BLUCK,

On Tuesday, April 17th, 1849, the property of the late H. R. Ince, Esq.,

COMPRISING three excellent feather beds, mahogany four-post and other bedsteads, night commode, bidet, washhand-stands, dressing-tables, chamber requisites, &c., excellent mahogany chests-of-drawers, large mahogany dining-tables, satin wood card, round, and other tables, lot of parlour chairs, easy ditto, excellent carpets, splendid mahogany secretaire with book-case and folding doors, celluret, small oak chest-of-drawers, handsome mahogany sideboard, weather-glass, writing-desk, work-boxes, pair of handsome decanters, cut tumblers, wines, breakfast and tea services, curious old china, plated candlesticks, silver cruet-stand, Palmer's candle lamp, handsome candle bracket, dressing-case, pole and curtains, draft and backgammon boards, couch, fenders, fire-irons, large quantity of books, including a Medical Library, large Bible, Imperial Encyclopaedia, Dictionaries, Boswell's Antiquities, Taylor on Philosophy of Aristotle, &c. &c.; three handsome chimney-glasses, very large superior French plates, fancy bellows, chimney ornaments, butler's tray, set of dish-covers, excellent eight-day clock, trays, kitchen chairs, fish kettle, quantity of bacon, five quarter casks, lot of excellent brewing utensils, pots, kettles, and other articles too numerous to mention.

On Wednesday, April 18, 1849,

WILL BE SOLD BY AUCTION,

By WALTER BLUCK,

In the Large Room at the RADNORSHIRE ARMS HOTEL, removed for convenience of sale from the residence of the late H. R. Ince, Esq., a valuable collection of

OIL PAINTINGS,

WATER-COLOUR DRAWINGS, PRINTS, &c.,

The property of J. M. Ince, Esq., who is removing to a distance.

No. CATALOGUE.—PRINTS.
1. Girl and Child.
2. Animal Affection ⎱ a pair.
3. Innocent Recreation ⎰
4. Trial of St. Stephen ⎱ pair after Smirke, R.A.
5. Christ before Pontius Pilate ⎰

WATER-COLOUR, CRAYON, AND BODY-COLOUR.
1. Flower Piece.
2. Baggage-waggon passing a Heath.—*Ince.*
3. Landscape—Shepherds and Sheep.—*Ince.*
4. Crayon Drawing—Moonlight.—*Bright.*
5. Malvern Church.—*Ince.*
6. Love's Dream.—*Wright.*
7. From "Humfrey Clinker!"—*Wright.*
8. Margaretta of Anjou, after Westall.—*Ince.*
9. Pair of body-colour drawings.
10. Pair of water-colour drawings.—*Ince.*

OIL PAINTINGS.
1. Sketch of a picture.—*R. Wilson.*
2. Portrait.—*Gainsborough.*
3. Portrait.—*Hopner.*
4. Rachael going to meet Jacob.—*Castiglione.*
5. Three sketches.—*J. Scarlett Davis,* and one of the school of *Bergham.*
6. Dutch river scene.—*De Koning.*
7. Near Hastings, looking towards Beechy Head.—*Vincent.*
8. Portrait of Opie, painted by himself.
9. Moonlight.—*Crome, junior.*
10. View of Norwich.—*Old Crome.*
11. From Scott's House of Aspin.—*J. West.*
12. Wood scene.—*Solomon Ruysdael.*
13. River scene.—*F. Watts.*
14. Landscape, with horses and heifer.—*G. Arnold, A.R.A.*
15. Lady Mary, sister of James, Earl of Berkeley.—*Lely.*
16. Christ with the hand on the globe.—*Morin.*

included five by Ince himself, of which *Baggage Wagon Passing a Heath* had been exhibited at the Society of British Artists in 1833. The oil paintings, however, show Ince to have been a discerning collector. Sometimes paintings were given in lieu of payment to an artist who had carried out a commission; but we can clearly see Ince's own choices as well. The sketch of a picture by Richard Wilson would certainly have been one that Ince bought, a late, highly esteemed, fellow artist of Wales. The Scarlett Davis paintings would have been given to him by his old friend, quite likely after Ince had advanced him a loan as the latter was nearly always in financial difficulty. There was a painting by John Opie (1761–1807), a British artist introduced in London as the 'Cornish Wonder', who was elected to the Royal Academy and painted many well known people including William Siddons, the actor, and who had a very good control of chiaroscuro reminiscent of Rembrandt. The list of artists also included Salomon Van Ruysdael (1602–1670), whom Ince admired greatly for his golden 'Dutch light', likewise de Koening. Gainsborough (1727–1788) needs no introduction and must have made a very good price, even in those days. Giovanni Benedella Castiglionoe (1616–1670) was known for his animal studies and mythical paintings. When he died he left some excellent etchings, also in the style of Rembrandt. Sir Peter Lely (1618–1680) was of Dutch parentage and came to London by 1647 and found fame as a portrait painter for Charles II after the Restoration. How Lely's portrait of Lady Mary, sister of the then Earl of Berkeley, came into Ince's collection, we will never know.

The Norwich School of Painters has been mentioned in an earlier chapter and Ince was one of their great admirers, probably visiting Norwich himself; we find no less than four 'Old Cromes' in the collection and one by Crome Junior. J.F. Herring's (1795–1865) *Cart Horses in a*

16. Christ with the hand on the globe.—*Marinari*.
17. Coast scene.—*John Wilson*.
18. Duck decoy.—*Old Crome*.
19. Landscape on canvl.—*Vincent*.
20. Sea piece.—*Vangoyen*.
21. Spanish port.—*Baptista Mula*.
22. Old buildings, Norwich.—*Old Crome*.
23. On the Thames.—*Ince*.
24. Landscape.—*Pinnie*.
25. Head.—*Ditto*.
26. Circular landscape.—*O'Connor*.
27. Edith finding the dead body of Harold.—*Hilton, R.A.*
28. Cart horses in a village.—*J. F. Herring*.
29. Horses in a stable.—*Ditto*.
30. Evening with cattle.—*C. Ward*.
31. Near Cromer.—*Vincent*.
32. Landscape.—*Hilder*.
33. Landscape, with dead tree.—*Ibbetson*.
34. Fruit piece.
35. Coast scene.—*G. Chambers*.
36. Capital landscape.—*Stark*.
37. Landscape with old ruins.—*Hilder*.
38. French fruit girl.—*Woolmer*.
39. Near Bromley, Kent.—*Sidney Percey*.
40. Gravelly banks.—*Old Crome*.
41. A scene in Venice.—*Canaletti*.
42. The Trespassers.—*R. B. Davis*.
43. Dutch galliotts bearing into port.—*J. Wilson*.
44. Portrait of a setter.—*Ince*.
45. Banditti.—*Ditto*.
46. Head of an Italian Brigand.—*J. Scarlett Davis*.

The items listed for sale by auction after the death of Dr. Ince, including some paintings entered into the auction by Joseph Murray Ince

Village shows Ince's love of horses again. Herring started life as a stage coach whip and achieved great fame for his horse portraits; he sold extremely well even then, for in a letter to his friend Stanhope, written only a year before Ince's sale, he says 'I sold a picture last year for which I received £157.10s, it was resold for 250 guineas and since for 500 guineas'. Even so, Herring's meticulous equine paintings were mostly carried out inside, which is why his hunting scenes have landscapes 'tame and poor, compared to the free play of wind and sunshine that David Cox put with easy vigour and joy into his painting scenes'.[7] Julius Caesar Ibbetson (1759–1817), a northerner from Scarborough, painted in London before going out to Java for several years as a draughtsman at the British Embassy. He made many interesting studies of country life and customs and his rustic figures and cattle paintings were full of zest and realism, and this could be why Ince admired him. The picture by 'C.' Ward (might one suppose this is a misprint and that he could be the famous James Ward, RA (1769–1859), George Moorland's (1762–1804) brother-in-law), was a painting called *Evening with Cattle*, again the farming background. Finally, a Canaletto (1697–1768). There was much of his work in England, partly from the fact that so many of the 'ton' (the Georgian 'In' set) by now had been to Venice and also that Canaletto himself had spent ten years (1746–1756) in England, mainly in London. He was the greatest 'Vedute' of his time (bringing topography into great Art). When Ince had first gone to Oxford and immersed himself in the scenes and the famous buildings, he would have studied the technique of Canaletto closely. In fact, in nearly all Ince's paintings there is the 'little red hat' or 'red jacket' willing the eye to the foreground of the picture, a practice much favoured by Canaletto.

This sale was of a rare collection of paintings and would that there were some details of where they all went afterwards. Surely some would have stayed in Radnorshire, if not in Presteigne itself.

8　The Final Years

It would appear that once Ince had dealt with his father's estate he went on a short European tour of his own — there is a study of *Tombs along the Appian Way* (plate 36), now in a private collection, dated 1849, and *The Alhambra* of the same year, showing that he also journeyed through Andalucia.

On his return he decided to move to Cambridge and took up residence at 12 King's Parade. He had found while working in Oxford that a university town was much to his liking, it gave him the opportunity of new friendships and of interesting intellectual discussion, which suited his new maturity. By now too, he felt that he had a strong enough reputation, especially after the patronage of Queen Victoria, to be sure of a ready clientele for any teaching. At Cambridge he was at the forefront of both scientific invention and new ideas. The *SS Great Britain* had been launched in Bristol in 1843; the first big railway terminal had been opened in London at St. Pancras; Louis Daguerre was producing photographs; an extraordinary means of communication called Morse Code was being used; Darwin's Theory of Evolution was now being accepted; Dr. John Snow had discovered that cholera was carried by polluted water and chloroform had been invented. There was to be better safety in the mines and the new tubular bridge over the Menai Strait had opened. In literature Dickens had just started his amazing series of books with *Oliver Twist* and Charlotte Bronte had published her *Wuthering Heights*. Alfred Tennyson was the Poet Laureate and in 1851 there was the Great Exhibition. It was not all good news however; potato blight had struck leading to famine in Scotland and Ireland. In London on 19 December 1851 Joseph Mallord William Turner had died, and Ince would have felt this as a personal loss.

So, Cambridge was now exactly right for Ince. It made him forget or at least come to terms with his own tragic loss. He enjoyed imparting the knowledge and experience that he had gleaned in his own search of painting and drawing. He liked teaching his students the language of art.

This university routine became part of his own life; it ran parallel with all the modern scientific thinking, and yet it was a link to the ancient classics, and philosophy. This is what he had found in nature. In painting creation which was as old as time, yet for ever changing and renewing itself, he knew it had demanded his whole, and he had accepted that with joy in the knowledge that this was the life he wanted. Now he felt a new affinity to the genius of those architects who had conceived these magnificent buildings in the city which had stood the test of time so valiantly. His interiors, too, are not just structures — they are charged with spiritual energy, and in the study and the sheer labour of drawing these he absorbs some of the simple faith of the artisans themselves.

Whilst Ince lived in Cambridge, he returned every year to Presteigne and Wales. However, his exhibitions in London were now sparse. In 1850 he showed *Old Ruin in farmyard at Chesterton, near Cambridge* in the Society of British Artists and at the British Institution *Kings College Chapel, the choir from the Screens*, now in the Fitzwilliam Museum. In this year he painted *Jack in the Green* (plate 13), a watercolour now in Hereford Art Gallery, and *Brecon, Presteigne* and *The Usk, Llangynidr Bridge* (plate 21) all in the National Library of Wales. In 1851 he painted *Newton Farm*, which had been the home near Brecon of Sir David Gam, the veteran knighted by Henry V who died at Agincourt, (his previous injury giving us the expression 'a Gammy leg'). Also that year he exhibited *Brecknock from the Castle Bridge with Honddu Mill and Bridge, the Castle, Old Cottage and Brecon Beacons*. The National Library of Wales also has two paintings of *Tintern Abbey* painted in 1853, together with *Stapleton Castle, near Presteigne*, a pencil sketch showing Baker's Farm when it was thatched.

Ince may have been to Edinburgh for a short time for he exhibited a painting called *Presteigne Church at Twilight* at the Royal Hibernian Society, Dublin from an address in the city. There is no evidence he actually went to Dublin for he could easily have sent the painting by 'steam packet'.

On his father's death, in addition to his role of executor, Ince had also taken on the position of legal guardian of his younger half brother. In 1851, Edward Ince Young was living with his mother in a house in Church Street. This may well have been the same cottage in West Wall in which Dr. Ince had died two years earlier. In the same census, Mary Young was able to describe herself as a 'retired servant', inferring that she was able to support herself and her son on his one-third share of the income of Dr. Ince's estate. Edward was described as a scholar, aged 14, and was probably attending John Beddoes School. Ince was presumably involved in the decision that Edward should be apprenticed to a manual trade, like his other nephews, the sons of Henry Ince. Ironically, in view of his uncle's artistic skills, Edward was apprenticed to a house painter. By 1861, Edward could describe himself as a 'painter (master)'

When Edward Young wished to marry Mary Powell in 1857, he was 19 years of age and still a minor and had to ask for his guardian's consent. The licence, dated 6 April 1857, was obtained in Presteigne from the Bishop of Hereford's representative, Edward having to swear 'that Joseph Murray Ince is the Guardian lawfully appointed of him the said Edward Ince Young and the person lawfully authorised to consent to the said Marriage and that the said Joseph Murray Ince is consenting to the proceedings of the said Matrimony'.

The marriage duly took place at St. Andrew's, Presteigne on 9 April 1857. Edward's wife, Mary Powell, was born in Presteigne in 1833 to John Powell and his wife Ann. John Powell had been a butcher at the time of Mary's christening on 20 October 1833, but was an innkeeper at the time of her marriage. Mary's mother, Ann Powell, signed the marriage register as a witness. The bridegroom signed the marriage register as Edward Ince Young. Shortly after the marriage, but before his first child was baptised in March 1858, he changed his surname to Ince.[1]

Some papers at the National Museum and Gallery in Cardiff show that Edward Ince and his family had in their possession several works of art given to him by Ince. In 1919, the director of the Museum was building up biographical detail on Ince, having just acquired several of his works for the national collection. He had heard that Ince's half brother was still alive in Presteigne and wrote asking for information. The reply dated 24 November 1919 still survives in the museum's files. In it, Edward Ince states 'I dare say there are many of his paintings in different collections. I have a few viz Carnarvon Castle in oil, gypsy encampment, &c.'

In 1923, the vicar of Aymestrey, the Rev. W.E. Johnson, wrote to the museum 'You may be interested to know … that a portrait of J.M. Ince … is in the possession of Mr. Ince, 35, Manor Rd, Stoke Newington, [London] N. 16.' The Mr. Ince referred to was Frederick Ince, the eldest son of Edward Ince. Frederick died on 18 November 1925 and in his Will made only a fortnight earlier he bequeathed 'to my brother Edward Ince such of my pictures as he may select'. Clearly there were some interesting works by Ince and also a further portrait of him which has yet to come to light.

Ince made his Will in January 1859, nine months before his death, and appointed James Edward Davies of the Middle Temple, Barrister at Law, and his lifelong friend, and William Price, draper of Presteigne as his executors, which covered both his London and country interests. The witnesses were A. Wall Davies, physician of Kington, (James' father); E.M. Tearne, surgeon of Presteigne, and Henry Griffiths, attorney's clerk of Presteigne.

He died on 24 September, 1859 back in London. His death certificate records the cause of death as 'Bright's disease, General dropsy and Anasarca'. Bright's disease is a term (now obsolete) for degenerative disease of the kidneys. Dropsy and anasarca, or oedema to use the modern term, describe the water-retention and swelling of the body's soft tissues that is a characteristic symptom of kidney failure. The disease had been first identified in the 1830s by Richard Bright, a doctor at Guy's Hospital in London. Ince's death was registered by C. Ince who was also living at 9 George Street. This is likely to have been his sister-in-law, Charlotte, the wife of his elder brother, Henry. Perhaps they were living with Joseph in his rooms and caring for him during his final illness. The 1861 census shows that they were still living in the vicinity, at 4 Newberry Place, St Pancras which is across Regents Park from George Street.

The *Hereford Times* of 15 October, 1859 gives him only a brief entry. 'Died on 24 September in London, aged 50, Joseph Murray Ince esq, artist of 9 George Street, Portland Square, London, and Presteigne,

Joseph Murray Ince
Artist
Who from early childhood to the close of life
was an inhabitant of this town.
Endowed with an ardent love of nature
his taste was cultivated and matured
under the guidance of David Cox
(that great master in the English School of landscape painting).
But although acquainted with the noblest scenes in Europe
he returned from foreign travel
to love anew the charms of this valley.
'Those fields, those hills - what could they less! had laid
strong hold on his affections were to him
a pleasurable feeling of blind love,
the pleasure which there is in life itself.'
For constant and intimate communion with them
he was content to abandon the exciting but arduous struggle
for a wide and enduring fame.
Combining, nevertheless, a rare industry with genius
the indulgence of his simple tastes
was linked with the 'certainty of honourable gain'
and in following his profession he acquired a considerable fortune,
which however he did not live to enjoy.
He died on the 24th day of September A.D. 1859
in the 53rd year of his age,
and was buried in the cemetery in Kensal Green

The wording on the memorial tablet to
Joseph Murray Ince in Presteigne church

Radnorshire'. Ince was, of course, 53 years old when he died, not 50, but the same mistake is made on his death certificate.

He was buried on 28 September, 1859 in Kensal Green Cemetery, in an area that is now designated as a 'wild area' (grave no: 15476/21/3). How very right that Ince should lie in an area of natural landscape. Kensal Green was then a popular and prestigious place for Londoners to be buried. Only a week before Ince's burial, the engineer Isambard Kingdom Brunel, who had had such a profound impact on the development of the Victorian transport system, was also buried there.

Ince's Will was proved promptly after his death on 11 November 1859. The value of the Estate was assessed as 'under £10,000', a substantial sum, and all earned by Ince's talent as an artist, as we know that he inherited little on his father's death. The memorial in St Andrew's church, Presteigne is correct in its summary of his finances – 'Combining, nevertheless, a rare industry with genius, the indulgence of his simple tastes was linked with "the certainty of honourable gain"; and in following his profession he acquired a considerable fortune, which, however, he did not live to enjoy'.

Ince left sums of £1,000 in 3% Government Stock to his brother Henry (on trust to pay the income of £30 per annum during his lifetime and that of his wife Charlotte), to his half-brother, Edward Ince Young, and to 'my nephews and niece (the sons and daughter of my said Brother Henry Ince) Thomas Ince William Ince and Susan Ince now wife of John Wells of Henrietta Street Covent Garden London'. These legacies totalled £5,000 in government stock but did not account for the whole estate.

The residue was to be divided equally three ways between 'my Nephew Francis Ince, Emma Phillips of Shrewsbury (sister of my late Wife) and Elizabeth Davis widow of Scarlet Davis Artist'. Based on the probate value of the Estate, there would have been about £1500 due to each of these three beneficiaries. In addition, they would eventually share the £1,000 held in trust for Henry and Charlotte Ince for their lifetime.

The identity of Francis Ince is an unsolved mystery. Oliver[2] suggests that there are three possible explanations: Ince may have had, besides Henry, another brother with a son called Francis; that his brother Henry had a son called Francis; or that Ince mistook the name of Edward Ince Young's first child, Frederick, who had been born on 7 February 1858. Oliver points out that there is 'a complete absence of any evidence' for another brother and rejects the second hypothesis as 'there is no record of such a son, and any reason for the artist treating one of Henry's sons differently from the others seems hard to come by'. He concludes that 'Francis' must be Frederick Ince, the child of Edward Ince Young.

His conclusion is not convincing. The first explanation can, however, be safely rejected. War Office records confirm that Dr. Ince had only two sons and corroborate their dates of birth.

It is not so easy to reject the second explanation. We know little of brother Henry and his family after their entry in the 1841 census in Presteigne, until their reappearance in London in the 1861 census. They were living in Dolley Green in 1843 when their daughter Harriet Ann was born. Henry himself was a witness at the marriage of his son William Henry Joseph in London in 1860. By the time of the 1861 census, Henry and Charlotte were living alone as all of their children had left home. It is unfortunate that no trace of the family can be found in the 1851 census, as this would make clear whether there was another child called Francis. Strangely at the time of the 1841 census, Charlotte was not at home in Presteigne with Henry and the 8 surviving children. The youngest child was 2 years old and it is possible that Charlotte was staying elsewhere on a temporary basis, either heavily pregnant or with a new-born child. Until the missing census entries can be traced, the identity of Francis Ince will remain a mystery but most likely he was an additional son of Henry Ince.

The identity of the other two residuary beneficiaries is clear from the Will. Emma Phillips, the sister of Ince's wife, Sarah, was born in Presteigne in 1824. Oliver[3] has fully researched the Phillips family and shown that the parents, Thomas and Elizabeth (née Cross), moved to Presteigne shortly before 1819. Thomas Phillips was a painter and decorator and ended his working life as caretaker of the Judge's Lodgings at the Shire Hall in Presteigne. The building is now a museum and has been restored to the condition in which it was in the mid nineteenth century. Thomas Philips died on 5 September 1845 aged 67 and his wife died on 21 February 1847 at the age of 66. They were buried in the same grave in Presteigne churchyard, very close to where their daughter, Sarah, Ince's wife, and their grandson, Henry Joseph, had been buried in 1835.

It seems that Emma Phillips was always a favourite of Joseph Murray Ince. As Miss E. Phillips, she was recorded as a subscriber to the *Seven Views*, although in 1832 she would have been only 8 years of age. Ince married her sister in 1834 and it is possible that they were already engaged to be married some two years earlier. Emma Phillips probably left Presteigne after her mother's death in 1847. In 1851 she was living with her elder sister, Mary, at 37, High Street, Shrewsbury, where they kept house for their brother, James. The Phillips brothers, James, Edward and William were partners in the firm of J.E. and W. Phillips (for which see p.65).[5]

By the time of 1861 census, Emma Phillips was her brother's only housekeeper at the house in High Street, Shrewsbury. She evidently put her inheritance to good use because she was able to retire to Llangollen. In 1881 she was living, still unmarried, at Berwyn House in Bache, near Llangollen. Her source of income was recorded in the census return as 'Dividends & Annuities'.

Elizabeth Jane Davis, the widow of Ince's friend, John Scarlett Davis, was the third residuary beneficiary. She was born Elizabeth Jane Abbot on 2 December 1815 and married Scarlett Davis on 12 July 1832 when she was only 16. They had six children, three boys and three girls, although only the girls survived beyond infancy. Scarlett Davis left no Will and little in the way of assets when he died in 1845. It would be typical of Ince's generosity that he should help his best friend's widow in this way and then make her future secure when he died.

Elizabeth Davis never remarried and died on 10 August 1874 of tuberculosis, aged 58. She would have received the initial portion of the residue (about £1,500) but did not live to collect her share of the £1,000 in trust for Henry and Charlotte Ince. Charlotte did not die until May 1877 and when news of her death reached a nephew of John Scarlett Davis, he wrote to James Edward Davis, Ince's executor on 1 August 1877 asking for £50 to be paid to him. It appears from the letter that Elizabeth Davis had received from him an advance of £50 in about 1867, which she had enjoyed interest-free, on the strength of her further expectation from Ince's Will.

One question which is raised by Ince's Will is why his elder nephews were not named as beneficiaries in it. The Will lists three of Henry's children — Thomas, William and Susan — possibly four, if Francis proves to be another child. Yet it excludes at least three other children who are known to have been alive at the time that the Will was made. The three sons are Henry Robert Ince (known as Robert), Edward Joseph Cowell Ince and George Sanders Ince.

Robert would have been 32 in 1859 and was probably living and working as a carpenter in London. His two eldest children were both born in London, Horatio, near Regents Park in 1855, and Joseph, in 1864.[5] While Robert cannot be traced in the 1861 census, the evidence suggests that he was then in London. We cannot, however, be sure of his status at the time.

Edward Joseph Ince would have been 30 in 1859 and was prospering in 1861. He had been apprenticed to a shoemaker and was working as such in Back Lane, Knighton when his daughter, Lavinia Janetta, was born in February 1861. When the 1861 census was taken in April, he felt confident in describing his status as 'Fundholder'. Clearly he had money in the bank and that could only have come from his uncle, Joseph Murray Ince. His prosperity appears to have been short-lived. He continued to work as a shoemaker in Knighton until about 1866, when he moved to Broad Street, Presteigne. He was still in Presteigne in 1871 but moved back to Knighton and died there on 10 November 1892. His widow, Jane, described him as a 'Shoemaker (master)' on his death certificate.

The story of George Ince is similar, although more sketchy. He was born in 1831 and so would have been 28 at the time that his uncle died. His trade is unclear as he cannot be located in the 1851 census. However, by the 1861 census, he was back in Presteigne, lodging at an inn in the High Street, and describing his status as a 'Gentleman'. He, too, must have had money invested on which he could live. George Ince surfaces next in the 1891 census, living in Dudley, Worcestershire, where he was working as a machine fitter.

It seems that both Edward Joseph Ince and George Ince came into money shortly before 1861, but when it was gone, had to revert to their trades to make ends meet. The only credible source of their wealth would be their uncle, Joseph Murray Ince. We may conclude that, knowing he did not have long to live, Ince not only made his Will specifying generous legacies to his younger relatives, but also made similar gifts in his lifetime to his older nephews, who were already established in life.

Appendix   What became of the Inces?

Descendants of Henry Robert Ince 1797–1869

Ince's brother Henry had made each of his sons learn a manual trade to earn their living. The eldest, Robert, was apprenticed to a carpenter, Edward and Thomas were both trained as shoemakers and George was a machine fitter. William, however, appears to have had no particular trade or profession as he described himself as a 'gentleman' when he married in 1860.

Robert Ince was working in Ryde on the Isle of Wight in 1866 and was living there with his family when his son George was born. Thomas had also moved to Ryde by 1869 together with his family. Their father, Henry Ince, was living with Thomas in Quarry Road, Ryde when on 8 March 1869, he died of pthisis, a condition related to tuberculosis. The death was reported by Thomas' wife, Fanny, who was present at the death. Henry's widow, Charlotte, continued to live with Thomas and Fanny in Ryde, and they named their sixth child after her when she was born in 1870. In all, Thomas and Fanny had nine children. It may have been due to lack of space in the house to which they moved in Newport, Isle of Wight or perhaps due to Charlotte's physical or mental condition, but she was moved into the Carisbrooke Workhouse. She died there on 16 May 1877 of 'age and debility' according to the death certificate.[1] It reveals that her son Thomas was present with her when she died.

A letter survives in the family papers of John Scarlett Davis,[2] the lifelong friend of Ince, which suggests that at the time of her death Charlotte Ince was still receiving the income from the £1,000 of 3% Reduced Annuities left to her and her husband for their joint lives. The letter, dated 1 August 1877, was written by a D.J. Davis to James Edward Davis, one of Ince's executors. In it he states that 'I received a letter this morning from Messrs. Batty and Whitehouse informing me of the death of Mrs. Ince (widow of the late Major Ince) in May last — by which the thousand pounds left for division by the late Mr. Ince of Presteign becomes available for that purpose.' John Scarlett Davis' widow was a residuary beneficiary of Joseph Murray Ince's Will but had died before Charlotte Ince. In the circumstances, her one-third share of the £1,000 as a residuary beneficiary would have become available for division between the beneficiaries of her own Will.

Robert's and Thomas' families remained on the Isle of Wight after the death of their parents. The censuses for 1881, 1891 and 1901 show how they began a dynasty of Inces which has lasted to the present day. There are currently six Inces still listed in the Isle of Wight telephone directory in Ryde, Gosport and Cowes.

Henry Ince's daughter, Susan, was living in London. She had married John Wells a widower aged 47 on 26 February 1853 when she was 23. The marriage took place at the Register Office in The Strand. John Wells' profession is stated on the marriage certificate to be 'picture dealer' and given that he was born in 1806 and was the same age as Ince, it is tempting to conclude that he acted as a dealer for him. Ince's Will identified Susan and John Wells as living in Henrietta Street, Covent Garden and at the time of the 1861 census, they were still living there at number 17. By this time, John Wells was trading as a jeweller. Could it be that the supply of pictures had ended with Ince's death?

William Henry Ince was just 20 years old in 1859 when his uncle died, leaving him £1,000. He was baptised William Henry but used the names William Henry Joseph. On 26 September 1860 he married Annie Bailey at St. Martin-in-the-Fields, Westminster and was able to describe himself as a 'gentleman' implying that he did not have to work for a living. The 1861 census finds William and Annie living in Gravesend, Kent at 6 Prospect Place, Milton. William then stated his occupation as 'house proprietor', but as there were no boarders or lodgers staying with them on that night so it is unlikely that they had opened a boarding house. It is more likely that he had used his inheritance to buy a few properties which he then let. The 1861 census was taken on the night of 7 April and William died only a few months later, on 23 June 1861 on the Island of Jersey, where he was temporarily residing. By his Will, made on 13 October 1860, shortly after his marriage, William left the whole of his estate to be held on trust for his wife Annie. He chose as his executors his brother-in-law John Wells, jeweller, and his father-in-law George Bailey, hotel-keeper. It shows that he must have kept in close contact with his sister, Susan, after the Ince family moved away from Presteigne.

Edward Ince was the only child of Henry Ince who remained in the Presteigne area for the whole of his life. He was baptised Edward Joseph but appears as Edward Joseph Cowell Ince on the birth certificate of one of his daughters. The Cowell name is a reference to John and George Cowell, executors of William Ince. By 1858 Edward Ince was working in Back Lane, Knighton and had married Jane Cooke from Ludlow. In that year, his first child, Edward James was born, to be followed by Lavinia Janetta in 1861 and William Henry in 1865. Lavinia died in 1865 and was buried in Knighton. Shortly afterwards, Edward moved his family to Presteigne as can be told from the birth of Ann Elizabeth (her grandmother's names) in the summer of 1867. This must have been a time of turbulent emotion for the family as Ann's birth was followed a few months later by the baptism and death of William in December 1867. The 1871 census records the family still in Presteigne, in West Wall, but by the time of the 1881 census they had returned to Knighton and were living in Russell Lane. Edward and his wife were still living there when he died on 10 November 1892. Jane survived him by many years, although she was short of funds and was reduced to taking in washing, being recorded as a laundress in the 1901 census.

Edward Ince was not mentioned as a beneficiary in the Will of Joseph Murray Ince, presumably because the artist had already given Edward his inheritance before he died. Ince left £1,000 of government stock to each his nephews Thomas and William and his niece Susan, and to his half-brother, Edward Ince Young, but did not include the older nephews, Robert and Edward. Edward, who described himself as a 'cordwainer' or shoemaker on his daughter Lavinia's birth certificate in February 1861, was able to describe his occupation as 'fundholder' in the 1861 census only two months later. The most likely explanation is that £1,000 of government stock had been given to Edward by his uncle so that the investment income it generated meant he was no longer wholly reliant on working as a shoemaker for his living. In his own mind, he felt able to claim the superior status of a 'fundholder'. Edward Ince must have enjoyed good relations with his uncle because the only known portrait of the artist belonged to him. It is now in the possession of Hereford Museum and Art Gallery (see front cover).

Ince's name lived on in two branches of the family — Thomas Ince, a beneficiary in Joseph Murray Ince's Will, named his first son, born in 1860, the year after the artist's death, Thomas Murray Ince; Edward James Ince, the elder son of Edward Joseph Cowell Ince discussed above, named his only son Edward Joseph Murray Ince.[3]

Descendants of Edward Ince Young 1836–1925

Edward and Mary had eight children, six boys and two girls, all born and baptised (with the surname Ince) in Presteigne. The eldest, Frederick was born in 1858, followed by Sarah Ann[4] in 1859, John Edward in 1861, Alfred and James (twins) in 1863, Edward in 1865, Mary in 1867, and finally Richard in 1869. John Edward, Alfred and Richard all died in infancy. All children were baptised with the surname Ince.

Edward Ince inherited £1,000 on the death of Joseph Murray Ince and afterwards enjoyed a good standard of living. The 1861 and 1871 censuses show that he could afford to employ a house servant. In 1861 she was Sarah Ann Davies, a 15-year-old girl from Discoed; in 1871, Elizabeth Pugh, aged 16, from New Radnor.

Edward was in business on his own account and employed other workmen, although the type of work carried out by his business seems to have changed over the years. The 1871 census describes his situation as 'Master House Painter employing Two Men' and he was still categorised as an employer in the 1891 census. His initial training was as a house painter and he appeared to regard it as his principal occupation. Certainly Ince described him as such in his Will made in 1859. However, he was described several times in the Presteigne baptism register as 'plumber' or 'plumber and glazier' and also stated his occupation in the 1881 census as 'plumber etc'. By 1901, he was able to state that he was a 'retired plumber' but by then he had begun a new career as Surveyor to the Presteigne Urban District Council. When his wife Mary died in 1907, he stated his occupation on her death certificate as an 'Inspector of Nuisances'. Like his own father, Dr. Ince, he was clearly a man of great energy, because he took the position of manager of the gas works in Presteigne when he was in his 70s. He died on 16 June 1925 at the age of 88, when visiting his son Frederick at his home in Stoke Newington, London.

He lived throughout his life in Presteigne, initially with his parents in St Davids Street and later with his mother in West Wall. On marriage, he and Mary moved to High Street where Frederick was born in 1858. By 1859, they had moved to Hereford Street where they remained until the 1890s. The 1901 census saw Edward and Mary Ince living at Roseland in Broad Street where Edward was still living as a widower when he died. This was the house in which Joseph Murray Ince had lived after his marriage and in which his only son, Henry Joseph, was born in 1835. It was the house in which both his wife and his son died later that year and from which he could look upon their grave in the churchyard across the road. It is ironic that the last Ince to live in Presteigne should choose that same house.

What became of the Ince children? The two daughters lived contrasting lives. Sarah Ann, the elder, must have had a good standard of education as she appeared in the 1881 census as a 'governess (school mistress)'. She never married and lived in Presteigne with her parents until her father's death in 1925. She then moved to Bideford to live with her brother Edward and his wife Caroline. After his death in 1942, she lived for a time in Dudley, Worcestershire, before moving to Scotland to live in Perth with her niece, Olwen Augusta Ince. Olwen had married Andrew Cairnie Miller in 1922 and Sarah Ince lived with their family until her death in 1952 at the age of 92.

The younger daughter, Mary, made an unfortunate marriage. Her husband, Albert James Fletcher Ruck, had begun his working life as a marker in a billiards hall in Hereford before he was 14 and seems to have got a taste for alcohol at an early age. He was the manager of a boot and shoe warehouse in Stourport when he married Mary in Presteigne on 5 August 1890. They had five children, two boys and three girls. The first child, Edward Chancellor Fletcher Ruck, was born in Stourport in June 1891. Albert then took the job of a boot and shoe salesman based in Lincolnshire. The next three children were born there, Dorothy Mary in Lincoln in 1893, Albert Frederick and Olive Mabel in Stamford in 1895 and 1897. The family moved to Shrewsbury in 1900 when Albert took over the tenancy of the Castle Inn in Beacalls Lane. Their youngest child, Margaret Vera was born there on 21 January 1900. Sadly, the stock in the pub proved too great an attraction for Albert and he died of cirrhosis of the liver on 17 September 1903.

Mary was unable to cope with raising the family on her own. It must have been a traumatic time for her. There was, of course, no social security or other safety net to fall back on in the early 1900s and so Dorothy was sent to Gloucester to Albert's parents; young Albert and Vera were taken into an orphanage in Wolverhampton; and Olive went to Presteigne where she was raised by her grandparents, Edward and Mary Ince.

Mary Ruck then showed determination and good business sense in rescuing her fortunes. She took over the station buffet in Craven Arms, and making a success of it, was able to obtain the concession for the refreshment rooms at the busier station of Dudley Town. After a few years in Dudley she was confident enough to take the tenancy of the Castle Hotel in Dudley (from 1911 to 1915), followed by The White Swan there (from 1915 to 1920). In 1920 she moved to the Tontine Hotel at Ironbridge which she managed from 1920 to her death on 13 January 1924 from influenza. The profitable business meant she could get her children back from their temporary situations. Her daughter Olive worked with her in the hotel businesses and her two sons worked close by in Dudley. Vera lived with her in Dudley and worked as a telegraphist for the Post Office in Birmingham. Only Dorothy appears not to have rejoined her.

The three sons of Edward Ince all appear to have had a good education and he seems to have decided that they should do better than the manual trades which had been chosen for him and for Henry Ince's children. It was a time when there was a dramatic growth in the number of white-collar jobs and the development of a 'middle class' carrying out clerical work.

Frederick Ince moved to London as a young man and by the time he was 23 was working as a commercial clerk in the drapery trade, as recorded in the 1881 census. He continued in this role until after 1901 when he set himself up as an agent (presumably a commission agent) working in drapery. When he died in 1925, shortly after his father, he was still working as an agent.

His younger brother Edward was started off in a similar direction. He was apprenticed to Henry Hoadley, a linen draper with a substantial business in Buckingham Palace Road, London and was living 'over the shop' when the 1881 census was taken. This must have been a thrilling environment for a boy from the sleepy town of Presteigne. Henry Hoadley himself was only 31 and employed a shop staff living on the premises numbering 29, all of whom were younger than him! The fun and games can only be imagined.

Edward Ince junior was a man of ambition and considerable ability. After completing his apprenticeship, he left the drapery trade and entered the Civil Service. Since 1870 admission to the Civil Service had been by open competitive examination and Edward was able to take advantage of his education and intelligence by passing the Civil Service entry exam. He entered the Department of Inland Revenue in 1887 and was posted to Stourbridge, Worcestershire, where in 1888 he married Caroline Clara Cutler. Caroline originated from Bristol but her family were in London in

1881 and she worked as a dressmaker. Her elder brother, Reuben was then working as a telegraph clerk within the Civil Service. It is possible that he and Caroline suggested to Edward Ince that he should enter for the Civil Service examinations.

Edward and Caroline were living in Amblecote, near Stourbridge at the time of the 1891 census. Edward was then an assistant officer in the Inland Revenue. Their first child, Edward Lindsay, was born in Amblecote, Staffordshire on 30 November 1891. Their second child, Edith Mary, was born in 1897 in Bridgnorth, Shropshire, presumably because Edward's duties had required a move to that town. The third and last child, Olwen Augusta, was born on 1 August 1899 in Criccieth, Caernarvon. By this time, Edward was working as an officer in the excise department, based in Criccieth. His next and final posting was to Perth in Scotland where he was responsible for excise duties payable by one of the major whisky distilleries. He worked in Perth from about 1905 until his retirement in 1925 after reaching his 60th birthday. He spent his retirement at Bideford in Devon where he died in 1942 at the age of 77, his wife Caroline having pre-deceased him there in 1940.

Their son, Edward Lindsay Ince, proved to be an outstanding mathematician.[5] He went to primary school in Criccieth and to secondary school at the Portmadoc County Intermediate School. He completed his secondary education at Perth Academy when his father's career moved the family to Scotland. In 1909 he went to Edinburgh University and read mathematics, graduating with first class honours in 1913. He played a full part in student life, being elected senior president of the students' representative council and convenor of the international academic committee.

He carried out research, first at Edinburgh University (1913–1915) where he was awarded a Doctorate, and then at Trinity College, Cambridge (1915–1917) where he was a Smith's prizeman, having been rejected for military service on medical grounds in 1915. However, he cut short his research at Cambridge in 1917 and took up a national service appointment. After the war, he lectured at Leeds and Liverpool, before embarking in 1926 on the task of building a department of mathematics at the new Egyptian University in Cairo. He was a great success but resigned in 1931 and returned home, because of concern for his daughters' education and his own poor health. 1931–2 saw him back in Edinburgh as a lecturer, followed by three years at Imperial College, London from 1932 to 1935. He then returned again to Edinburgh University where, as head of department for technical mathematics, he remained until his death on 16 March 1941 from leukaemia.

In 1923, Edward Lindsay Ince was elected a fellow by the Royal Society of Edinburgh; late in his life he was awarded its Makdougall Brisbane prize but did not live to receive it. He was also a member of the London Mathematical Society and the Royal Astronomical Society. In short, he had a most distinguished career.

Edward Ince's other son, James, was put to work in the retail trade like his elder brother. He began work as a grocer's assistant in Presteigne, then moved to Swansea where he was working as a grocer in 1891. According to family tradition, he emigrated and all contact with him was lost.

The Ince family in London

Charles Ince was the cabinet maker son of William Ince but is a shadowy figure after 1800 when he took over his father's business. His son, Charles Vogel Ince was born in 1798 and so was seven years older than Ince. Charles Vogel married a first cousin, Isabella Cowell, on 20 May 1828 at St. Pancras Old Church. Isabella was the daughter of Isabella Ince, daughter of William Ince, and of George Cowell, his executor. We lose track of Charles and Isabella Ince after their marriage and they do not appear to have had children.

It is the descendants of another uncle, Frederick Ince, a grocer, who created a dynasty of Inces in and around north London. Frederick and his wife Martha (née Debar) had at least five children and it is the youngest two sons whose progress is followed here. The elder of the two, Edward Bret Ince, was born in Lambeth, probably in 1808. His baptism took place at St. Mary's, Lambeth on 16 October 1808. His younger brother, Percy, was born on 31 March 1818, although his christening did not take place until 28 November 1824 at St. Pancras Old Church.

Edward Bret Ince began in trade as a bookseller, specialising in legal texts. He had an entrepreneur's instinct and recognised that the marketplace was changing. The 19th century saw a growth in the number of lawyers and with the increase in legislation and litigation, the legal profession needed an accurate and timely form of law report. Edward Bret Ince took over as publisher of *The Law Journal*. He worked hard at building the list of subscribers and seems to have travelled the country ceaselessly in pursuit of sales. It is significant that he was not at home when any of the 1851, 1861 and 1871 censuses were taken. (In 1871 he was in Manchester on the night when the census was taken, describing himself as a 'law publisher'.) By 1881 he had retired from active business and the census for that year found him at home, when his status was 'retired traveller'.

Edward Bret Ince had married Ann Finnie on 24 January 1829 at All Souls, Marylebone. They had four children, three boys and a girl. The eldest, Henry Bret Ince was born on 3 November 1829 when the family were living in the parish of St. Pancras. The second child was Edward Percy Ince, born on 20 March 1834. The family had moved closer to the law courts in Chancery Lane by the time that their daughter, Catherine was born at Quality Court, Chancery Lane in 1837. The third son Francis was born on 6 August 1841 at 30 Robert Street in Hampstead, showing that by the 1840s the family could afford to move to the more attractive new suburbs that were being built. About 1850, the family moved to the St. Pancras area, but then returned to Hampstead, living first in Belsize Road and from 1870 until the late 1880's in Albion Road. Edward and Ann Ince both died there, he on 13 October 1886 and she on 11 September 1889.

Edward Bret Ince saw that the legal profession was a passport to financial gain and opened up possibilities of advancement that would not otherwise be available for his children. All three sons worked in different areas of the law. The eldest, Henry Bret Ince, was educated at London University[6] and began work in shipping before he suffered an accident which meant he had to change career.[7] He learned shorthand and began to work as a reporter, rising to become a leader writer on the *Daily News*. In November 1852 he was admitted to the Inner Temple as a pupil barrister and was called to the bar in 1855.[8] For a time, he continued to work as a legal reporter for The Jurist. In 1858 he published an authoritative study of the Trustee Acts of 1852 which remained in print for several years. In November 1859, at the age of 30, he switched to Lincoln's Inn and became a successful barrister in the Equity Courts. He had a reputation as an advocate for his enterprise, tact and perseverance. In 1875 he took silk, becoming a Queen's Counsel, and practising at the Chancery bar. He became a Bencher of Lincoln's Inn in November 1878 and was a member of the Bar Committee, indicating his standing within his profession.

Once established in his legal career, Henry Bret Ince took up a career in politics. He stood successfully for the parliamentary seat of Hastings in June 1883 until the general election of November 1885 when he was returned as an MP for the constituency of Islington East. This was the time of the controversy over Irish Home Rule. Ince was a Liberal and a firm supporter of the Gladstone government on the issue. The *Times* of 2 June 1886 reported his arguments in the House of Commons in favour of Gladstone's bill to give Ireland Home Rule. His position did not go down well with the electors of Islington and he was defeated in the snap general election of August 1886, called following the defeat of Gladstone's bill.

Almost three years later he was taken ill while working in his chambers in Lincoln's Inn and died of a brain haemorrhage on 7 May 1889 at the age of 59. Probate records show that he left a substantial sum — £19,784 — to his family.

His younger brother, Edward Percy Ince, started work as a clerk in the Court of Bankruptcy in Chancery Lane. The 1851 census shows that he was then aged 17 and living with his parents at 67, Albert Street, St. Pancras. Soon afterwards, he emigrated to Australia, where in 1855 he married Elizabeth Holloway, another migrant from London, at St. Phillips church in Sydney. He was then 21 and she was 30. They had two children while in Sydney, a boy who died at birth in 1856 and a daughter, Elizabeth Ann, in 1858. The family returned to London before 1861, when the census found Edward working as a journalist and living in Holborn. A second son, Percy Bret Ince, was born in 1861 but died the following year. A second daughter, Catherine Aylett Ince was born in 1863.

The tragedy that was to follow for the family illustrates how 19th-century families had to resolve matters for themselves in the absence of social assistance. On 13 November 1867 the *Times* reported the bankruptcy examination of 'Ince E. P., Masborough-road, Brook-green, reporter' was to take place on 27 November. Worse was to come. In 1868 Edward died of tuberculosis and was followed in 1869 by his wife Elizabeth, who also died from TB. There were two orphaned daughters aged 11 and 6 as a result. The elder daughter, Elizabeth Ann, was taken in by her grandparents, Edward Bret Ince and Ann, and lived with them until her marriage in 1885. The younger daughter, Catherine Aylett, was adopted by her uncle, Henry Bret Ince and as his Will shows, was regarded on an equal footing with his own children. Sadly she died in 1880 and did not live to enjoy her prospective inheritance.

Henry Bret Ince had married Annie Jane Gray Muggeridge, the daughter of a prosperous hop merchant from Twickenham in 1862. They had ten children, three sons and seven daughters. The three sons all followed their father into the legal profession. The first two, Bret Ince, born 1864, and Gerard Cranworth Ince, born 1865, were educated at Westminster School and Trinity College, Cambridge before being admitted to Lincoln's Inn as pupil barristers. Bret was called to the bar in 1887 but did not make his career there. Instead, he gained an appointment as Secretary to the Royal Commission on Vaccination in 1889 and held the post until 1897. In 1906 he joined the London staff of the Cambridge University Press and spent the rest of his working life there. He held the position of General Manager from 1924 until his retirement in 1929 at the age of 65. Gerard Cranworth Ince was called to the bar at Inner Temple in 1889 and practiced in the Admiralty Court. Their younger brother, Cecil Henry was educated at Bradfield School in Berkshire and chose to qualify as a solicitor rather than a barrister. His wife, Florence Elise Welton, whom he married in 1893, was the daughter of a solicitor from Woodbridge in Suffolk. There can be no doubt that this family had the law in its blood!

Francis, born in 1841, was the youngest of the three sons of Edward Bret Ince. In 1861 he was a solicitor's articled clerk and in 1865 qualified to practice as a solicitor. He was a remarkable man who built a legal firm bearing his name, which still prospers today. He was no narrow lawyer, but had a fascination with photography and a passion for science, particularly in the then new field of electrical engineering. His father had wanted him to have a modern education and entered him to the Metropolitan School in Gower Street, London, a secondary school which did not just teach the traditional classical syllabus, but specialised in mathematics and science. Edward Bret Ince sent all his sons to the same school, which he had previously attended himself.

In 1866, only a year after qualifying as a solicitor, Francis Ince moved to Cardiff to take up a partnership with John Ingledew, practicing as Ingledew Ince. In the 1860s, Cardiff was one of the fastest-growing towns in the UK. Its prosperity was based upon coal and at its peak, it was the world's biggest coal-exporting port. No doubt the trade provided numerous lucrative shipping disputes for the lawyers of Cardiff. Francis Ince rapidly made an impact in Cardiff in shipping and commercial law cases and Ingledew's firm which made £500 in 1865, the year before he arrived, made £6,000 in 1868.

Ingledew's London agent was a Mr. Bennett, with whom Francis had served part of his time as an articled clerk. When he dropped dead in his office in 1869, the clerks telegraphed Francis and asked him to return to London and take over the practice. Ingledew was supportive and two firms were established, Ingledew Ince and Vachell in Cardiff and Ingledew Ince and Greening in London. Ingledew retired in 1880 and the partnership between him and Francis Ince was dissolved. The London firm was now to practise as Ince and Colt.

Francis Ince and his family lived in Alexandra Road, Hampstead before moving to a large house on the Chelsea Embankment, opposite Battersea Park. The success of his legal practice enabled him to buy a country estate, The Hermitage at Jarvis Brook near Rotherfield in Sussex. He would spend weekends and holidays in the country, eventually retiring there. He died at Rotherfield in November 1920 at the age of 79. He had made his fortune through his legal practice, leaving an estate of £79,858.

In 1865 Francis Ince had married Zoe Buisson, the daughter of a French emigré, Jean François Buisson, born in Pau in about 1797. Francis and Zoe had nine children, four boys and five girls. Two of the boys, Gerard Buisson Ince, born in Cardiff in 1866, and John Oscar Ince, born in 1874, practiced as solicitors. Both joined their father in the partnership, but neither made much of a mark. Gerard, the eldest son, was a partner from the 1890s until 1907, when he retired on ill health grounds. He subsequently lived in warmer climates in the south of France, in Almeria in Spain, and finally in Tunisia where he died in 1942. John trained as an engineer but then made a major change of career, training as a solicitor and being admitted as a partner with his father in 1900. The firm's name was changed to Ince, Colt and Ince in recognition of there being two sons in partnership with their father.

The firm continued to prosper, with a series of able partners being recruited. It became the leading London firm in shipping law and has held that position until the present day, now practicing as Ince & Co. It has succeeded in developing an international network of offices in locations such as Piraeus, Hamburg, Le Havre, Hong Kong, Shanghai and Singapore. To date, Ince & Co is the only ever recipient of the award of Global Shipping Law Firm of the Year. It is a testament to the strength of the legacy of a remarkable man.

Francis Ince also left his mark on electrical engineering. It was as a result of his initiative in recognising the need of electrical engineers for formal training that the Electrical Standardising, Testing and Training Institution was founded on 1 January 1890. The Institution was best known for its Faraday House training college in London which, before its closure in 1967, produced a succession of leading engineers, including six Presidents of the Institution of Electrical Engineers.

Francis' reputation as a practical lawyer, with a knowledge of electrical science, gained him a major client and, in the long run, a son-in-law. One of his friends, Alfred Thompson, an engineer, met a 17-year-old inventor, fresh from school, who was working for the British arm of Siemens Brothers. He had made his first commercial invention — an arc light for street lighting — when he was only 13. The youth was Sebastian Ziani de Ferranti who had developed an electrical alternator containing several revolutionary features. Thompson wanted him to get good legal advice on protecting his invention and took the youth to meet Francis Ince. Francis was impressed and advised Ferranti that, with his unique talent, he should leave Siemens and exploit his own inventions; if he did not do so, his employers would pay him well — but only as an employee, and keep the profits of his inventions for themselves.

By the end of 1882, Sebastian had established Ferranti Thompson and Ince Ltd. to exploit the Ferranti-Thomson alternator. The foundations were laid for the growth of Ferranti Ltd. in the 20th century. During Sebastian's lifetime, (he died in 1930), the company's range of electrical products included generators, transformers and cables for power stations, domestic appliances, radio components and electric meters. The company was always innovative and subsequently led the development in Britain of computers, microelectronics and avionics. It was a household name for most of the 20th century and remained under the control of the Ferranti family until 1994, when it ceased trading following a disastrous American acquisition.

Francis Ince regularly invited Sebastian de Ferranti to his London home to dine with the family and also travelled with him to meetings on the Continent, sometimes accompanied by one of his daughters. One in particular, Gertrude Ruth, who had been born in Cardiff in 1869, soon made sure that she was her father's first choice. After several meetings with the young inventor who was five years older than her, romance blossomed. They were married in 1888 at St. Dominic's, Haverstock Hill in Hampstead when Gertrude was still only 18. They set up house initially in London, but Sebastian moved the company's main factory from London to Hollinwood near Oldham in 1896. The family home was established at Baslow Hall in Derbyshire in the early 1900s and remained there until his death in 1930. Gertrude wrote a charming account of her life with Sebastian and published extracts from his letters shortly after he died.[9]

Gertrude was assisted in writing the book by her youngest brother, Richard Basil Ince. By 1934 when it was published, he was making a living as a writer. It had been a long journey, with several dead ends, before he found his true vocation. Richard was born in 1882 and never enjoyed the scientific and mathematical emphasis of his education at the Metropolitan School, his father's old school. His autobiography, published in 1932, describes his childhood with an irascible and possibly overbearing father. He was left weakened by a serious childhood illness and never enjoyed the best of health. His father, Francis, used his business connections in shipping to obtain a clerical post for Richard in the offices of a shipping line. But he was bored by the work and made too many mistakes, and decided that his career lay in the Church and his father agreed. He went to Peterhouse College, Cambridge where he studied for a history degree, graduating in 1906. He then studied at Wells Theological College later in 1906 before being ordained a deacon in 1907 and a priest the following year, both ceremonies taking place at Peterborough Cathedral. Richard accepted a curacy in the parish of Higham Ferrers with Chelveston and Caldecott in Northamptonshire. He stayed two years before moving in 1909 to Holy Trinity, Fareham. He only stayed for a year and by this time, he had concluded that the priesthood was not, after all, his vocation. His health was poor and he returned to live with his parents.

He recognised that he had the creative urge and began to write. A few stories were accepted for publication in newspapers and a book of poems, *The White Roads and other verses*, followed in 1916. His career did not flourish until the 1920s when he wrote biographies of Mesmer, Joan of Arc, and Martin Luther. Later factual work included *A Dictionary of Religion and Religions* (1935) and a biography of John Donne (1939). He wrote several novels which earned him a steady income although none of them were best-sellers. Richard Ince published three novels in the 1960s after a long fallow period. He died in 1969, aged 87, at his home in West Meon, Hampshire.

Richard's eldest sister, Ada Catherine Ince was born in Cardiff on 3 February 1868 (when Francis Ince was practising law there). She had inherited the Ince family's creative genes and chose to train as an artist at the Slade School. She exhibited a picture at the Society of Women Artists in 1896,[10] but then owing to failing eyesight, she had to abandon any thought of pursuing a career as a professional artist. She took up painting once more when in her 60s and achieved some success. In October 1936 there was an exhibition of her flower paintings at Walker's Galleries in New Bond Street, London. Adrian Bury wrote an appreciation of her work:[11] 'Her method of sketching direct with a large full brush, drawing at once in colour, is well suited to the emotion she feels in the presence of flowers. Properly to interpret a rose requires great concentration, for its aspect quickly changes, and if the artist lingers too long over the details, something of the freshness of leaf and tint must elude the brush. Miss Ince, by constant practice, has taught herself to select the essentials of her flowers and to eliminate unnecessary facts, giving a broad, and in some cases, extraordinary sense of form and colour.' There is a collection of five of her flower paintings, dating mostly from 1937, at the Brighton Museum, a bequest when she died on 21 September 1954 at the age of 86.

Returning to Percy Ince, the youngest child of Frederick Ince and Martha Debar, he worked as a commercial clerk for over 30 years, for a time for a publisher. When he was in his 70s, he became a commercial traveller. Percy married Sarah Winkworth on 24 July 1843 at All Souls, Marylebone and together they raised six children, three boys and three girls. The eldest son, Percy Edward, born in 1846, became a solicitor's clerk but died in 1865 at the age of only 19. The second son, Charles Frederick, born in 1850, began his working life as a clerk but managed to set himself up in business as a stationer. From small beginnings, his firm flourished and expanded into printing and (eventually) into publishing, becoming a limited company as C F Ince & Sons Limited. The 'sons' were three of his five sons, who in due course became directors of the company. Two of the sons worked full-time in the business but the third, the eldest son, Charles Percy Ince, was never fully involved.

Charles Percy Ince was an artist by profession, specialising in water-colour landscapes, particularly of marine subjects. He was born on 10 June 1875 in Hackney and educated at Cowper Street Boys School off City Road, Islington before taking a degree at King's College, London. He began his working life as a bank clerk but evidently had ambitions to become an artist and chose to become a pupil of Henry George Moon. Moon was an interesting choice of tutor. He had been born nearby in Barnet in 1857 and studied at art school, but had to support himself by working in a solicitor's office. No doubt he could identify with the young bank clerk whose heart was set on becoming an artist.

Moon's opportunity had come in 1880 when one of the most influential gardeners of the time, William Robinson, invited him to become an artist for the periodical *The garden*. Thereafter, Moon made his reputation with his beautifully coloured and outstandingly accurate botanical illustrations. The plates that he produced for Frederick Sander's monograph on the orchids, *Reichenbachia*, published from 1888 to 1894, represent his highest achievement. In the later part of his life, Moon concentrated more on landscape painting, while still producing plates for *The garden*. He exhibited eight watercolours at the Royal Society of British Artists and a further nine works at the Royal Academy. The majority were landscapes in Essex or Hertfordshire, but some flower illustrations were shown at the Royal Academy. He died in St. Albans at the age of 48. Robinson wrote an obituary of Moon in *Flora and sylva* and paid tribute to his skills: 'His powers as a pure colourist were remarkable, and depended on his knowledge and experience of wet colours, and the exact effect they would have on dry paper'.

Charles Ince began to exhibit at the Royal Society of British Artists in 1912 and was elected a member of the RBA in the same year. This society remained his principal interest and in all he exhibited 198 works there during his lifetime. He also exhibited regularly at the Royal British Institution (being elected a member in 1927), the Goupil Gallery, the Glasgow Institute of the Fine Arts, the Royal Academy and elsewhere, on an occasional basis. He painted mainly in watercolour but also in oil, exhibiting a few times at the Royal Institute of Oil Painters. His subject was never far from water and included a range of sailing vessels (yachts, tugs, drifters, schooners and barges) and waterside features such as watermills, bridges, warehouses and boat-houses.

He lived with his parents in Purley, Surrey until 1923 when he married Norah Gozney from Shireoaks in Nottinghamshire. He was 47 years old and she was 25. They set up home in Nyewood, near Bognor, Sussex and their only child, Mary Norah Gertrude Ince, was born there in 1927. In 1933 they moved to Fareham and then the following year to Southsea, both in Hampshire. In 1937 they made their final move to Purbrook House in Purbrook, Hampshire, where Charles Ince died on 8 July 1952.

He does not appear to have travelled far from home to judge by the location of his paintings. There were trips into Huntingtonshire and Lincolnshire, Dorset and Cornwall and one to France — taking in Avignon and St. Tropez. Otherwise, the landscapes painted were within a short distance of home, with views of Arundel and Littlehampton from the years at Nyewood and subjects in Porchester and Bosham painted when living in Purbrook. A typical picture is the watercolour *Dredging the Mouth of the Adur* which was exhibited at the Brighton Art Gallery Autumn Exhibition in 1926. It was purchased for the Gallery's collection and can be seen there today.

Bibliography

Colver, Dr. R. *The Welsh Cattle Drovers*, University of Wales Press, 1976.

Cox, T. *Cox the Master*, 1946.

Dickes, W.F. *The Norwich School of Painting*, Jarrold & Sons, 1905.

Hobbs, T. *John Scarlett Davis, a biography*, Logaston Press, 2004

Howse, W.H. *Presteigne Past & Present*, Jakemans Ltd, 1945.

    School & Bell, H. Parks Ltd, 1956.

Murchison, R.I. *The Silurian System*, John Murray, 1854.

Parker, K. *A History of Presteigne*, Logaston Press, 1997.

Rennell of Rodd, Lord *Valley on the March*, OUP, 1958.

Sparrow, W.S. *British Sporting Artists*.

Thornbury, W. *J.M.W. Turner*, 1862.

Williams, Revd. J. *A General History of the County of Radnorshire*, compiled from the Manuscript of J.A. Williams by Edwin Davies of Brecon, The Hereford Times, 1905

Transactions of the Radnorshire Society.

Transactions of the Woolhope Naturalists Field Club.

Endnotes

CHAPTER 1

1. This is confirmed in *A History of the Royal Berkshire Militia* by E.E. Thayts (1897), which shows a commission to Henry Robert Ince of Westminster to be Ensign in April 1793. (Published by the author at Sulhamstead Park, Berks., 1897).
2. *Ibid.*
3. 'Joseph Murray Ince (1806–1859), Artist of Presteign, Radnorshire' by R.C.B. Oliver in National Library of Wales *Journal* Volume XVII, (1972), pp 371–391.
4. According to the *Grand Armorial de France*.
5. The parish register records the mother as 'Mary' the wife of Henry Ince.
6. see note 3 above.
7. It has not been possible to prove that Sergeant-Major Henry Ince's family connection, but the existing evidence supports the notion that he was. He appears to have been responsible for the construction of the tunnels in the Rock, known as The Notch, which provided secure stores, strategic gun emplacements and places of refuge even when closely bombarded by enemy ships. He was a founder of the Methodist church in Gibraltar, donating the land on which the church was built. In 2004 the Ministry of Defence were selling off properties in Gibraltar, one of which was called Ince's Farm. It appears that this Ince was a Cornishman as he joined the Royal Engineers in that county. He was subsequently promoted to Lieutenant and married 'Jenny' by whom he had six sons and one daughter. He retired to Gittisham in Devon.
8. Edward Jenkins junior also became a JP and DL and owned the Grove, a lovely house on the Discoed road from Whitton near to Maestraelow. Edward married Margaretta, the only child of the Revd. John Jenkins, who was the rector of Knill and 'Perpetual Curate of Whitton'. They had only one child, Rosa, who married

Joseph Alfred Bradney of Tal-y-coed, FSA, JP, DL and Sheriff of Monmouth, thus the named line of the Jenkins family came to an end and Mrs Bradney inherited the estate.

CHAPTER 2

1. Lipscomb, writer and traveller in 1799 notes 'the civil face of our landlady at the Radnorshire Arms, and the civilities received from all compared with that in England, was highly disadvantageous to our own countrymen'!

2. *Salmonia or Days of Fly Fishing by an Angler* and dedicated to William Babington MD FRS notes: 'The green drake are descending on the water and some are leaving the alders to sport in the sunshine. ... The fly you see is called the Alderfly and appears in large quantities before the mayfly. It is brown and grey and very pale.' Colin Wilocks *The New ABC of Fishing* (p.165) notes: 'For hundreds of years fly fishing in Britain was an elementary sport — in that anglers were aware of only two or three of the common water flies — but by about 1850 observation, equipment and the development of the fly fishing art extended the original few flies to over a dozen. ... In the past Welsh anglers used to differ their patterns according to which wild flowers were in bloom. ... Day flies Olives, (in Welsh called the Blue Dun), Iron Blues, March Browns, pale wateries, mayflies and Blue-winged Olives.'

3. There were no 'Christmas trees', but a Yule log was always brought in, a great deal of greenery and a 'Kissing Bunch' hanging, made with mistletoe.

4. This pencil sketch and those on pages 18, 21, 30 and 40 are taken from a small leather-bound sketch book held by the National Museum and Art Gallery of Wales. Inside Ince has written: 'J.M. Ince 1829. Pupil of David Cox. Welsh Scenes.'

5. *The House of Cornewall* by Foljambe and Reade (1908).

6. Thayts *op. cit.* p.290.

7. The Meyricks, referred to in *Burke's Peerage* of 1887 as the 'Purist and noblest Cambrian blood' had as an ancestor, Cadafael, himself a descendent of Urien, Lord of Rhigid in AD 90. Cadafael warned Llewelyn the Great of impending invasion by the English by a marathon run over the mountains, carrying a lighted firebrand. For this Llewelyn the Great rewarded him with a coat of arms that included firebrands, the chough that inhabits the clifftops of Anglesey from whence the family came, all with a black background to represent night. Sir Gelly Meyrick, having fought in Flanders and sailed with Drake to the Azores, lived at the Court of Gladestry, some 7 miles west of Presteigne near Dolyhir. Unwisely he allied himself with the Earl of Essex in an abortive uprising against Elizabeth I which not only cost him his life but also his family their considerable estates.

8. His portrait, by John Wood, hangs in government buildings in Colombo.

9. The Rodd is a fine Jacobean mansion, the name of which is derived from Old English for a clearing. The first references to it are in the 13th century. The Rogers family and their Herefords are remembered in verse:

> Aaron Rogers at the Rodd
> Has got a bull, a living God,
> You will know the bull when his name is called
> The beautiful Sir Archibald.

10. A sad fact is recorded that although Samuel Stephens who was clerk of the Radnorshire Turnpike Trust, died in 1862, his sons Samuel Junior who had been in the Accountant General's Office GPO, London had died earlier of T.B. in 1842, as did his brother John Stephens, assistant in the Radnorshire Turnpike Trust and would have followed his father, but died of the same scourge in 1844.
11. Edited by Leslie A. Marchand (John Murray, 1973).

CHAPTER 4
1. Gainsborough referred to portrait painting as 'this cursed face business'.
2. W. Thornbury's book on Turner provides a description of the artist by Leslie, a friend and contemporary: 'Short and stout, with a sturdy, sailor like walk. There was that keenness of expression in his eye only seen in men of constant habits of observation.'

CHAPTER 5
1. PROB 11/742 at the National Archives.
2. *Dictionary of English Furniture Makers 1660–1840* edited by Geoffrey Beard and Christopher Gilbert, (The Furniture History Society, 1986), p.78.
3. *Ibid.*, p.589.
4. PROB 11/1522 at The National Archives.
5. See 'The Partnership of William Ince and John Mayhew 1759–1804' by Pat Kirkham in *Furniture History* (1974), the Journal of the Furniture History Society, Volume X p.56.
6. *English Looking-glasses. A Study of the Glass, Frames and Makers (1670–1820)* by Geoffrey Wills (Country Life, 1965), p.31.
7. The main details of the career of William Ince are taken from *The Bombay Artillery. List of Officers Who Have Served in the Regiment of Bombay Artillery from its Formation in 1749 to Amalgamation with the Royal Artillery* by Col. F.W. Spring (William Clowes & Sons Limited, 1902).
8. The will has survived in the records of the East India Company, together with the details of his personal effects and other possessions sold in Surat on 16 January 1809 at IOR/L/AG/34/29/343 and IOR/L/AG/34/27/388 pp.28-32 at The British Library.
9. IOR/L/MIL/12/139 Accounts Current with the Estates of Deceased Officers dated 1 May 1809 at The British Library.
10. See the Bill of John Prickett, surveyor, to William Ince, Churchwarden, and the Overseers of the Parish of Hornsey. Ref DRO/020/H/73 at London Metropolitan Archives.
11. PROB 11/1403 at The National Archives.
12. PROB 11/1453 at The National Archives.

CHAPTER 6
1. The British Institution (1806-67) was established as a rival to the Royal Academy at Boydell's Shakespeare Gallery in Pall Mall, and was aimed at encouraging and rewarding 'the talents of the Artists of the United Kingdom'. It also organised loan

exhibitions of Old Masters for students to copy. The Society of British Artists, based in Suffolk Street, was founded in 1824 by a rebel group of artists including B.R. Haydon, John Martin, John Glover and Thomas Heaphy (its first President). It became 'Royal' in 1887 while under the Presidency of Whistler. The Royal Academy had been founded in 1768. In spite of its rivals the RA was, during the Victorian period, at the zenith of its power and prestige, and its exhibitions were the high point of the artistic season.

2. As shown in *The Story of P & O* by David and Stephen Howarth (Weidenfeld & Nicholson).

3. There is an interesting reference of the *Transactions of the Woolhope Club* when Sir Roderick was elected an honorary vice president a few years later. He said in his speech at the age of 16 he had had the honour of carrying the Colour of the 36th Regiment at the battle of Vimara. The Duke of Wellington was just behind them at the charge and expressed himself delighted with the steadiness of the men in making it. 'His Grace in fact, devoted a whole paragraph in one of his despatches to a description of the charge of this single regiment. Two thirds of the men at that battle were actually natives of Herefordshire — this memory was one of the reasons why he felt such an interest in this beautiful part of the country' (Applause!).

SECOND COLOUR SECTION

1. Colours given by Ince as: Morning: 'Sky cobalt, White, Yellow ochre, Lt. Red, same for distance only deeper, same colour blended together for Cottage. Trees & banks on right side. Trees on left with black, yell ochre & cobalt scumbled with Bone brown & antwerp blue & little brown pink high lights adding a little patent yellow Some Brown antwerp blue for water adding white for high light. Little lake and white for pinky heath. Yellow ochre for high light on Rocks, others [?], clouds white & touch of patent yellow.'

For Evening: 'Sky. Cobalt, Lt. Red, Yellow Ochre & white. extreme distance same only little deeper and warm yellow in sun light – yell ochre and black for first ... [?] of foreground bank bushes etc. with white forming Greys for earth stone steps fallen tree warmed with yell ochre, Raw Sienna & Burnt Sienna, Bone brown and brown pink Glaze Bone Brown & antwerp Blue. Water same with yellow ochre. Little touch of Burnt Sienna to warm earthy bank. Grey of cottage Red yell ochre. Burnt Sienna warm, cow, Bone Brown. Yell Ochre middle cow. Black, white yell [?] cow Lt. Red. Black White distant cow patent yellow high light, also with yell. ochre Black figure yellow ochre ... [?] on foreground vegetation.'

Artists in Ince's day had no 'tubes' of ready mixed paints and no synthetic colours. That was to come with the Impressionists. There were no laws against using poisonous substances either. *Green* was achieved by mixing black with yellow ochre; *Bone Brown* was made by from calcified bones and was good for glazing as a light brown — great expertise was needed for allowing the first layer of glaze to dry and building it up with subsequent layers; *Antwerp Blue* was the forerunner of Prussian Blue, but a much paler version; *Patent Yellow* had a high degree of oxycloride of lead and was very poisonous — but a beautiful, clear light yellow. (*Notes on the technique of painting* by Hilaire Hiler (Watson Guptil)).

Ince's actual texts that accompany the paintings *Morning* and *Evening* respectively

CHAPTER 7

1. W. Thornbury's book on J.M.W. Turner notes that 'a tree is only a tree with Gainsborough, yet with Turner it is a willow or an oak.' This is also true of Ince, as can bee seen by these intelligent and sympathetic studies.
2. Ince chose to exhibit at several art society exhibitions, particularly at the Society of British Artists. The Royal Academy had a rule prohibiting artists from being candidates for associate if they exhibited with any other society. Ince may have decided that he was achieving sufficient success and did not want to jeopardise it by restricting himself to exhibiting only at the Royal Academy.
3. Oliver *op. cit.* p.374.
4. *A History of Presteigne* by Keith Parker (Logaston Press, 1997) p.127.
5. At RG 9/122 101. The head of the household is recorded as 'George' Ince, but the birthplace of Wendover, Bucks and occupation 'Lieut in the Army' make it clear that he is Henry Ince.
6. *The Victorian Watercolours and Drawings in the Collection of H.M. The Queen* by Delia Millar (London, 1995).
7. *British Sporting Artists* by Walter Sparrow (Bodley Head, 1922).

CHAPTER 8

1. Under English Common Law, a person may change their name without making any formal record, provided there is no fraudulent intent. The use of a deed poll made before a solicitor is the best-known type of formal record, but a statutory declaration sworn before a JP or Commissioner of Oaths would be equally effective. Some deed polls were enrolled for safekeeping in the Close Rolls of Chancery but no

record exists of most changes of name in the period. At present, no formal record of Edward Ince's change of name has been traced.

2. Oliver *op. cit.* p.382.
3. Oliver *op. cit.* pp.382-4.
4. Oliver *op. cit.* p.383.
5. The choice of names for Robert Ince's sons lends support to the view that the Francis Ince who was a beneficiary of Ince's Will was indeed a further son of Henry Ince. Robert's brothers or, to put it another way, Henry's younger sons, were named Edward Joseph, George, Thomas, Horatio and William. Robert named his sons Horatio, Joseph, George and Francis William. The similarity in the names chosen suggests that Robert had a further brother named Francis.

APPENDIX

1. The death certificate is registered in the name of 'Mary Ann Charlotte Ince', but the identity of the deceased is clear as her occupation is recorded as 'Widow of Henry Ince a Lieutenant in Berkshire Militia'.
2. I am grateful to Tony Hobbs for a copy of the letter.
3. Spelling as recorded on the birth certificate. GRO ref Births Sept quarter 1887 Cardiff registration district 11 a 375.
4. The record for Sarah Ann, baptised on 29 November 1859 shows what may have been the formal position after Edward Ince's change of name. The father's christian names are recorded as 'Edward Ince Young' and his surname as 'Ince' .
5. *Oxford Dictionary of National Biography* ed. H.C.G. Matthew and Brian Harrison (Oxford University Press, 2004). It gives a good account of the life and work of Edward Lindsay Ince at Vol 29, pp.218 – 219.
6. *Who's Who of British Members of Parliament, Vol 1, 1832-1885* by Michael Stenton (Harvester Press, 1976) p.206.
7. Obituary in *The Times* 9 May 1889 p.11.
8. The Records of the Honourable Society of Lincoln's Inn Vol II 1800–1893, Lincoln's Inn (1896) p.289.
9. *The Life and Letters of Sebastian Ziani de Ferranti* by Gertrude Ziani de Ferranti and Richard Ince, (Williams and Norgate, 1934).
10. *The Dictionary of British Artists 1880–1940* compiled by J. Johnson and A. Grentzner, (Antique Collectors Club 1978) p.268.
11. Walker's *Monthly* October 1936.

Index

Cox, D., training under 31, 35-36
Dictionary of Artists of the English School, entry in 1
Dictionary of National Biography, entry in 1
Edinburgh, in 90
exhibiting 1826-37 57-59, 66, 68, 77
       1842 77
       1844 78
       1847-48 84
       1850 90
family, financial responsibility for 75, 76
fishing, love of 12-13
French background 2-3
influences on 37-42
marriage 65-66
Oxford, in 66
Will 76
Sarah (wife) 65-66, 67
Susan Wells (niece) 93, 98
Thomas (nephew) 93, 97
family of 98, 99
William (grandfather) 4, 43, 44-50, 54
The Universal System of Household Furniture 47-48
William (uncle) 50-51
William (nephew) 93, 97, 98
Ince & Mayhew (furniture makers) 45-50

Jenkins, Dr. Edward 6, 85
family of 6
Mr. 72
Johnson, Revd. W.E. 91
Jones, Anna Maria 52
Jones-Brydges, Sir Harford 71
Whitcombe 71

King, James 38
King-King, James 28
Kington church *21*

le Jeune, Comte 2
Lely, Sir Peter 87
Lewis family of Harpton Court 27
John 27
Harriet 29
Robert 27, *28*
Thomas 27
Linnell, John 35

Maria, James de 32
Marshall, Benjamin 41
Mayhew, John 45-50
Meredith, Edward 30
Meyrick family 24
        Edward Stanton 24-25, *25*
        Thomas King 24, *24*
Mitton, Nancy 23-24
Murchsion, Sir Roderick 63
        The Silurian System 63-64, *64*

Nant-y-Groes 6
Norman, Samuel 45
'Norwich School, The' 41, 87-88

Oliver, Mr. R.C.B. 2, 3, 4, 93
Opie, John 87
Owen, Mr. Huw 3

Palmer, Samuel 35
Parsons, Cecil 29, 71-73
Phillips, family of Shrewsbury & Presteigne 65
        Emma 93, 94, 95
        Robert 16
        Sarah 65-66, 67
Poole, Miss 34
Powell, mary 91
Presteigne 10-12, 24-30, 30
        Beddoes / Grammar School 15-17
        curfew bell 176
        family move to 6, 9
        flood of 1838 76-77
        folklore 19-22
        medical practice in 9-10
        Radnorshire Arms 72-73, *73*
        Roseland 30
        Warden Court 30
Price, William 92
Prout, Samuel 35
Puget, Admiral Sir Peter 26
Pugh, Elizabeth 100

Ragg, Mary 32
Reynolds, Sir Joshua 38, 39
Rodd, The 29

Pictures mentioned